JUDAISM AND ISLAM

POPULAR JEWISH LIBRARY

Prepared by the World Jewish Congress

Edited by Chaim Pearl

First Series: published by Lincolns-Prager

THE PARTING OF THE WAYS A. Cohen
THE LAND IN WHICH GOD DWELLS Edmond Fleg
WINSTON CHURCHILL ON JEWISH PROBLEMS Oskar K. Rabinowicz
THE VISION WAS THERE Franz Kobler
CONTEMPORARY YIDDISH LITERATURE A. A. Roback

Second Series: published by Lincolns-Prager

HISTORY OF ANGLO-JEWRY Israel Finestein
THE STORY OF THE ALEPH BETH David Diringer
IN SEARCH OF HOME AND FREEDOM Arieh Tartakower
AN INTRODUCTION TO JEWISH LAW P. Elman (Editor)
THE DUAL IMAGE:
  THE JEW IN ENGLISH LITERATURE Harold Fisch

Third Series: published by Thomas Yoseloff

A GUIDE TO HASSIDISM H. Rabinowicz
AN INTRODUCTION TO JEWISH
  BIBLE COMMENTARY Bernard M. Casper
THE ESSENCE OF JEWISH ART Ernest Namenyi

JUDAISM AND ISLAM

*   *   *

ERWIN I. J. ROSENTHAL

LONDON   THOMAS YOSELOFF   NEW YORK

Printed and made in England by
Fletcher and Son Ltd Norwich and
the Leighton-Straker Bookbinding Co Ltd London

CONTENTS

AUTHOR'S NOTE

The following book has been written for the Popular Jewish Library series of the World Jewish Congress not as a piece of scholarly work for the specialist, but for an interested general reading public among Jews; for people who want to know something about the relationship between Judaism and Islam. I have tried to set out the fascinating story of this interrelationship as accurately as I could without becoming too much involved in technicalities. I could not, in the nature of things, quote chapter and verse for factual statements nor, to my regret, acknowledge in the usual way my indebtedness to the many scholars and their numerous books, monographs and articles which I have used in the preparation of these pages. All I can do is to acknowledge my debt in general and refer the reader to the select bibliography at the end. Many of the books listed there contain valuable bibliographies for reference and further study. I hope that those of my readers who have found it worthwhile to follow this account will go for fuller information on matters in which they are interested to these studies.

In dealing with a subject so wide and intricate one is forced to be selective. I can only hope that I have not left out anything of material concern to the story as a whole.

ERWIN I. J. ROSENTHAL

INTRODUCTION

The meeting of Jews and Muslims in the Middle Ages produced one of the most interesting and important epochs of
Jewish history. Its significance and relevance for Judaism and
the Jewish people to our own day can hardly be exaggerated.
The talmudic age apart, there is perhaps no more formative
and positive period in our long and chequered history than
that under the empire of Islam from the Mediterranean to
the Indian Ocean.

Under medieval Islam, the foundations were laid for the
systematic interpretation of Judaism. Hitherto undreamed
of opportunities for self-expression, for a full and rich
flowering of the Hebraic genius were matched by grave
dangers to the very existence of Judaism. For the first time
since the end of Jewish statehood the scattered Jewish communities, coming under the rule and influence of an ex-
panding, militant new faith, found themselves confronted
by a religious civilisation which advanced the same exclusive
claim to possessing not only the whole truth but also the
only right way to its realisation in an all-embracing discipline. The challenge of Islam, once it had consolidated
itself and grown to maturity—thanks largely to Jewish ideas
and institutions skilfully adapted to Arab needs—was much
more dangerous and powerful than that of Christianity
which had sprung from Judaism. It was also more alluring
and persuasive than that of Hellenism—important elements
of which it had absorbed. For Islam as a system of
beliefs, convictions and of conduct was much nearer to
Judaism. It claimed to contain the same divine revelation in
Arabic through Mohammed. It was also—and this should
not be underrated—the faith and practice of a conqueror

who held effective power and authority and controlled the lives and fortunes of its protected Jewish minority.

Spiritual kinship and political astuteness, born of necessity, combined to allow large-scale participation in the emergent and rapidly developing Islamic culture and civilisation to its second class 'citizens'. In theory, only the Muslims as members of "the community of the faithful" enjoyed in law and life the full rights and privileges of the ruling majority in a far-flung empire, while minority groups suffered legal disabilities. But in practice, non-Muslims were free to observe their religion, whether they were Jews, Christians, Sabeans or Zoroastrians. Their communal autonomy was extensive enough to allow them wide scope for development and expression alongside the Muslim majority with whom, outside the strict religious area, they fully shared in all spheres of life, economic, social and cultural. Without them, the organisation and administration of the empire, the smooth functioning of government, of trade and commerce, as well as the flowering of intellectual life and of personal well-being would have been impossible. In making this big claim we must naturally remember that converted Jews (and Christians) played an important part in the development of Islam. This is the more understandable since in Islam as in Judaism there is, apart from the strictly political and economic activities and functions, hardly any manifestation of human life independent of the all-embracing discipline enshrined in the minutely defined religious duties.

There is, to our tidy Western mind, a certain contradiction in this claim of the all-pervading rule of the religious law. It is obvious that this claim often remains in the realm of theory, but it persists as the ideal demand issuing from the freely accepted truth of revelation. Zeal and vigilance of the appointed or self-appointed spiritual leaders of the community determine the degree, at any given time in history, of realisation of the ideal demand in the daily lives of majority and minorities alike. Rigorous application of the religious all-embracing law makes for segregation, stresses the superiority and power of the dominant faith, discriminates against those excluded from the "community of the faithful" through their stubborn refusal to convert and to conform. The rigidity and fanaticism of the purists provoke a similar attitude among those who are second-class members of society. This is amply attested by the extensive polemical literature, as we shall see later.

The fact remains that the Jews participated in a kindred culture and civilisation which by far surpassed in depth and spiritual power anything they had known since the days of Hellenism. The Jews adopted the Arabic language of their conquerors and with it many a form and quite a few ideas. And yet, despite all assimilation to the Muslim mode of life and to Muslim ways of thought, the Jews under Islam maintained, even enriched, their distinctive character as Jews with a vigour and determination hitherto unknown.

Now was the time to define and describe Judaism with a clarity and force unique in the whole history of the Jewish people. The basic tenets of Judaism, its formative concepts and ideas, were combined into a system intended to sustain the Jews, to demonstrate their distinctiveness, to secure survival and to instil hope and expectancy of redemption. The form of this exposition was largely borrowed from Muslim theology and religious philosophy. Even the newly developing codification of the *Halachah* and the *Responsa*-literature of the Geonim owe their form to Muslim patterns.

The following pages will show that this borrowing was slight compared with the many ideas and institutions and customs the Muslim religion took over from Judaism. But we are not concerned with percentages, we do not draw up a balance sheet so that we can nurse our pride and establish gratifying proof that we have imparted much more in quality and quantity than we have accepted. What matters is that there was mutual give and take, the very existence of communication, a communication by no means confined to the goods of the world to sustain the body. True, much of this communication of the mind took the form of controversy: it shows that both sides were alive, that it was more than a battle of pens, a theoretical exercise divorced from the everyday life of peoples and civilisations. It was a struggle for the soul of men whom history had thrown together; and it says much for the vitality of Judaism and for its adherents who displayed fearlessly the courage of their convictions that the challenge was met and that Judaism emerged purified and strengthened and enriched to such an extent that it could bequeath a meaningful intellectual and moral legacy to Christian Europe. It matters little that the classical heritage had been filtered through the religious attitudes of Muslims and Jews and had been assimilated and modified in the process to make it acceptable to the ethical monotheism of its recipients and adaptors. On the contrary, only in this strange garb could it weave Greek and Hellenistic ideas, concepts and institutions into the fabric of our much vaunted Western civilisation.

Only a closely knit community devoted to such a complete guide through life as Judaism offered in *Halachah*, and *Aggada*, in Bible, Talmud and Midrash, could withstand the powerful onslaught of a vigorous, land-hungry people which was sustained and bound together by the new faith of Islam. For Islam could claim, with much more justice than Christianity, to have superseded the *Torah* and its rule over man's entire life. Yet, thinkers and teachers arose who had the power to formulate the essentials of Jewish belief and practice in such a way that neither force nor persuasion could entice a vanquished Jewry away from their ancestral faith. But for this ability to present Judaism not only as equal, but as superior to the new religion, the Jews living under Islam could never have made their signal contribution to the new civilisation which was destined to affect Europe so powerfully. On the other hand, the up-to-date presentation of Judaism at the same time enabled the majority of Jews to withstand the spiritual and material inducements of a brilliant civilisation and to hope for an end to the Exile and for a speedy redemption. Attraction was more than balanced by opposition and determined rejection, as is amply attested by an unusually rich and varied literature in Arabic and Hebrew, much of which has unfortunately not yet been made available to our own generation. The Hebrew Bible apart, this literature in all its ramifications has no peer in subsequent periods of Jewish history.

Needless to say, there are many problems which life in the Diaspora at a later stage shares with an earlier age. But no period reflects them more clearly and more classically than that spanned by the encounter between Judaism and Islam from the 7th to the 17th centuries. There was never more similarity between a tolerated Judaism and its adherents and a civilised, masterful overlord until the post-emancipation period. Hence, there was never a greater opportunity for integration nor a greater danger of assimilation. It was precisely that tension between participation and aloofness, that belonging to two worlds with fewer mental reservations, than at any other time before the modern age, which enhanced Jewish creativeness, clarified Jewish distinctiveness and produced a less unequivocal delineation of Jewishness within otherness.

At the same time, it achieved a definitive concept of *Galut* or Diaspora Judaism which is relevant to our own problems. This must not blind us, however, to the basic dissimilarities between that epoch of Jewish existence and our own. Fundamentally, the great divide is the changed attitude to religion. No matter how widely certain concepts and customs differed between Muslims and Jews, basically they were at one in their unquestioning faith in divine revelation in the form of a prophetic law of perfect truth, eternal validity and complete sufficiency for man in this world and the next. Both religious groups had the same concept of the universe with God in the centre.

Many of us moderns no longer share such a faith, and the existence of the State of Israel which, in any case, does not alter our attitude to other faiths, powerfully affects our will to Jewish survival. But whether the modern Jew is a strict believer or not, it can hardly be claimed that Judaism is the sole motivating force of his every thought and action, that it is his central authority. This may or may not be due to the general change of attitude to religion, to faith in God. We certainly see emerging—and not only in the State of Israel— a sort of secular Judaism, a historical-cultural affirmation of identification, of belonging.

This new attitude is by no means confined to the Jews, it has penetrated deeply into Islam under the impact of Westernisation. Oversimplifying greatly, one could say that the Jew-Muslim relationship has been replaced by the Jew-Arab and Israeli-Arab relationship. But this is by no means so simple and clear cut a replacement and a division. It is not easy to determine what force Islam is and what power it has today in the various national States, even where Islam is the State religion. But we must realise that Jewish-Muslim affinity and opposition can and will be used as occasion demands in deciding political questions of war, truce or peace, of hostile or peaceful co-existence. Pan-Islamism and Pan-Arabism are twin brothers. It is obvious that political aspirations count far more than theological niceties. But it is equally clear that an accommodation which leads to normal peaceful relations cannot be achieved on the basis of political and material self-interest alone. It is here that appeal to spiritual values, to affinities of a common and shared civilisation is meaningful and potentially helpful. This is the more important when we realise that to have ceased to believe in Allah and his law does not mean abandoning the cultural heritage of Islam, the Muslim code of behaviour, any more than Jewish agnosticism means turning one's back on Jewish ethics. On the other hand, we cannot take for granted an automatic reopening of the fruitful co-operation between Jews and Muslims which characterised a thousand years and more of living together under the rule of Islam. A conscious effort is needed on both sides to understand the common ground that once bound them together and to build on that knowledge and realisation a bridge of goodwill as independent, fully equal partners in a region which was once possessed of a culture common to both and capable of mutual toleration and beneficial working together.

At the moment, the chances of any agreement on whatever basis, material or spiritual, political or cultural, seem rather slender. The strength or otherwise of the Muslim consciousness will largely determine whether or not long-term self-interest will bring the Arab states nearer to Israel. On the Jewish side, more than a return to the ancient homeland, more than a physical return to the cradle of the religious Semitic civilisation is needed. One of the preconditions for a positive solution of the present conflict is at any rate the conscious realisation on both sides that to a large measure they share a good deal of common ground in the religious ordering of their lives in the past, and that much of their cultural achievement in the past springs from the same spiritual roots. The spiritual and the political climate

B

of our day may not be propitious for such mutual re-appraisal—as this hackneyed phrase goes—yet to become aware of one's roots is the first step for believer and agnostic alike on both sides towards forging a new link for the future on a basis more solid and stable than political expediency and material aspirations.

To trace the contribution of Judaism to Islam—on the basis of much research carried on over the past hundred and thirty years and beginning with Abraham Geiger—may, therefore, be more than an academic pastime, at least for those on both sides who can detach themselves from the day-to-day political struggle and can look beyond the more pressing problems of the moment, such as mere physical survival, defence and security, to the time when they dare daydream of a more humane life in an ideal world of sweeter reasonableness.

Let us, then, proceed to a brief survey of what Judaism contributed to the birth and development of Islam.

Part One

★

JUDAISM IN ISLAM

JUDAISM IN ISLAM

★

A few preliminary general remarks may not be out of place
in this context. Considering the place and time of the emergence of Islam it is well to remember that where religious
belief is concerned man often reacts to the numinous or
holy in identical or at least similar ways. The reason for this
lies as much in his rational as in his emotional nature. In a
very real sense we are children of one Father (though this
may manifest itself more in how we harm each other than
in how we obey our Father). It seems, therefore, futile to
look for and find influence where none really exists. While
it is legitimate and even necessary for the scholar to trace
ideas and institutions to their origin and to show their
development in a diversity of forms, it does not really matter
so very much whether something which is, for example,
common to both Judaism and Christianity has found its way
into Islam from the one or the other. This is the more so
since Arabia, the cradle of Islam, not only belongs to the
same Semitic world so prone to the manifestations of the
genius for religion, but also numbered among its inhabitants
both Jews and Christians.

It has often been remarked that there is little if anything
original in substance in the leading ideas of Islam. They can
all be traced to Judaism or Christianity, normative or
sectarian. But, viewed as a whole, Islam is not simply the
sum total of one or more of its predecessors. The genius of
Mohammed, its founder, has mixed the various ingredients

in such a way that something new, something fresh, different from its sources, has emerged. A strong personality, full of confidence in his mission, determined, single-minded, cunning, and treacherous where the Jews are concerned, created out of well-established ideas and concepts a new world-faith which his dynamic successors imposed in quick succession on one country after another which fell to their advancing armies. Had it been otherwise, Islam would have shared the fate of many a Jewish or Christian sect.

Although much of his preaching ran counter to Arab ways of thought and life, basically it appealed to a contemporary religious longing among the Arabs, winning enough influential support to let Islam prevail in Arabia and spread far and wide abroad. It was, therefore, less the matter borrowed than the manner in which Mohammed presented it to his Arabs that counted. The material was transformed in his hands to suit the temperament of his countrymen and to meet a particular situation in Arabia. The social and economic situation was no less favourable to Mohammed's message than the spiritual unrest. To underline the latter he relentlessly warned against the impending divine judgment which could be met and possibly averted only by a radical break with the prevailing paganism and by the exclusive worship of and devotion to Allah.

THE KORAN

What gave him this idea? Who were his teachers? Most likely, they were Jews even though the preoccupation with the Last Judgment was more pronounced among Syriac Christian monks. The idea itself, coupled with that of resurrection, is, naturally, genuinely Jewish, and Mohammed's obsession with it may just as well be due to his evaluation of the deplorable religious situation in Arabia. This much is certain, that the *Suras* of the Koran assigned to his Meccan period are full of references to Moses and his book of which Mohammed's own book is only the confirmation sent to the Arabs in the Arabic tongue. The fact that Mohammed not only reiterated a former revelation with which men to whom it had been sent acquainted him, but produced it in pure, clear Arabic, legitimised him as a prophet in his own right. He insisted on this since his opponents taunted him that he only repeated what had been recited to him by others who were human like himself. It is a moot point whether he sought their company in order to learn about the One true God and His demands so that he could be His apostle to his Arabs, or whether his Jewish associates tried to convert him to their faith.

Professor Goitein holds that considerable missionary activity was carried on by the Jews in the whole of Arabia; he sees in Deuteronomy 18. 18 : "I shall raise up for them a prophet among their own brothers" not only the pattern for Mohammed's claim that to every people a prophet had come "who was a brother of them", but also the reason why these Jewish missionaries gave up the idea of converting the Arabs to Judaism and concentrated instead on Mohammed.

In any case, it is clear that at first Mohammed looked upon himself and his message as in no way different from the prophets of other peoples, in particular Moses and the children of Israel. He naturally expected the Jews of Arabia to acknowledge him as the seal of the prophets and his message as the authentic revelation of the one God of justice and mercy. This attitude also prevailed in Medina after his flight from his native Mecca until he realised that the Jews of Medina would not embrace Islam in place of Judaism.

THE JEWS OF ARABIA

Much of our knowledge about the Jews in Arabia, apart from some inscriptions and tombstones, comes from Muslim sources. They, like the Christians, spoke Aramaic—a further reason why it is sometimes difficult if not impossible to decide whether a word and what it stands for has come into Islam from Jews or Christians. Recently, Himyaritic inscriptions from southern Arabia have come to light which confirm that long before Mohammed there were Jews and Judaised Arabs who worshipped one God, called *Rachman*, a term familiar from talmudic literature as a designation of God. Jewish settlement in Himyar probably goes back to about 200 C.E. whereas in the North, in the Hejaz, it dates back to the destruction of the Second Temple. They not only lived in towns, but also in villages and oases; they were organised in tribes and were, according to H. Z. Hirschberg, farmers growing vines, olives, and date palms, merchants and craftsmen who lived amicably with their Arab neighbours, whom they taught. They had produced poets and it seems that among their 'clients' were not only pagan Arab tribes but also converts to Judaism. A considerable number of *Kohanim* or priests seem to have settled both in northern and southern Arabia (Yemen) since Muslim historians refer to Yathrib, the later Medina of Islam, as a city of *Kohanim*. In the Koran, Mohammed calls their learned men *aḥbār*, a literal translation of the Hebrew title *chaverim*.

When Mohammed had failed to win the Jewish tribes for his new religion, he made cruel war on them, and they had to pay with death or exile for their refusal to join him. Many Arabs, and especially those in friendly relations with these Jewish tribes, deplored Mohammed's treachery, which he committed only after he had become strong enough to revenge himself on the Jews. At first he had welcomed the

Jews of Medina as allies, and in the "Statute of Medina" they figure as an *umma* who form, together with the "believers" the "*umma* of Islam". All members of this community stood in a relationship of *dhimma*, mutual protection, to one another.

This term *dhimma* underwent an interesting narrowing down to protected, second-class members of society, being later restricted to the "people of the book". From that time, the *dhimmis* were no longer obliged to share with the 'believers' in the burden of *jihād*, holy war against the infidels, nor naturally were they entitled to a share in the spoils of war. Against payment of *jizya*, poll-tax, and *kharāj*, land-tax, they were guaranteed the free exercise of their religion and were given communal autonomy, subject to certain restrictions, for instance, Jews were forbidden to build new synagogues, but were permitted to keep in good repair existing ones—which must not exceed in height the mosques. They must not blow the *shophar* to call their faithful to attend service. They were not allowed to ride on horseback, to drink wine in public, to accompany their dead with dirges and wailing. Most irksome of all was the injunction to wear distinctive clothing, a badge, a belt and coloured head-gear. The enforcement of these restrictions varied with time and place. On the whole they were not rigidly enforced, or at least not all together, except in sectarian Muslim States, as for example in the Yemen until all Yemenite Jews were flown to Israel. The same restrictions applied to Christians. Their chief aim was to humiliate the *dhimmis* and to mark them off visibly from the 'believers'. Despite a broad tolerance and a relatively secure, seldom endangered life, Jews and Christians were looked down upon with contempt.

Modern Israel, by opening its gates wide to its Oriental brethren, has done much to reduce the number of Jews

living in Arab states at the present time. In theory, the Jews
there are full citizens with the free exercise of their religion
constitutionally guaranteed them, even where Islam is the
State religion. It is mainly the absence of peace and friendly
relations between Israel and the United Arab Republic and
Iraq which endangers the position of Jews in these countries
and exposes them to the charge of Zionism and consequent
punishment and discrimination. But quite apart from these
politically motivated hazards, religious issues hardly enter
the picture, due mainly to the changing importance of
Islam in the rapidly changing pattern of life in the Muslim
Arab States.

JEWS IN EARLY ISLAM

In considering Mohammed and his teaching, we must bear
in mind how closely the question of the Jewish connection
of Islam is bound up with the relationship of Jews and Arabs
on a personal level. For it is important to know that
Mohammed was acquainted with Jewish teachings not by
reading the Bible, Talmud and Midrash, but through serious
conversations with Jews. We have to distinguish between
Jewish material in the Koran going back to Mohammed
himself and in the commentators of the Koran who not
infrequently make intelligible what is rather cryptic in
Mohammed's words. Much of what we find in the Koran
and its commentaries undoubtedly comes from Jewish converts to Islam, and most of the institutions and customs
which show Jewish origin and bear a close resemblance to
corresponding institutions and customs in Judaism, probably
go back to converts who were familiar with them through
their own observance while Jews.

Here again we note the great change that came over
Mohammed in his attitude to Jews. As has already been

stated, the "people of the book" are cited for corroboration and as authority in his early period. But there is a growing tendency after he has convinced himself that the Jews will not acknowledge him as the apostle of God who brought the final revelation superseding the *Torah*, to warn his followers explicitly not to do as "the people of the book". Hence, we find that in many cases the imitation of Jewish ways has gradually given way to modification and outright rejection. This is naturally only partially Mohammed's work; most of it took place after his death in the course of the development of Muslim law which went parallel with the spread and consolidation of the new religion. In the first century of the *Hijra* (the Muhammedan era dating from the flight of the prophet to Medina) converts were still coming in appreciable numbers to the new faith, notably in Iraq, the then spiritual centre of Jewry and the scene of the elaboration and consolidation of the *Halachah* or talmudic law under the geonim. While it may be surprising to find learned Jews defecting from Judaism and exchanging it for Islam, that this happened can hardly be doubted when we study Muslim legal enactments and customs raised to the level of obligatory religious law. What Jews would never have achieved by proselytism, apostates managed to do by the imposition on Islam of a number of important Jewish ideas and institutions.

The growing opposition to this judaizing tendency is reflected in a deliberate departure from or rejection of Jewish laws and customs. It stems not only from Christian converts to Islam, but also from the Arabs themselves and the Persians who were playing an increasingly important part in intellectual and religious life and in government and administration. It is possible, for instance, that the restrictions imposed on *dhimmis* mentioned earlier, wongly attributed to Omar I (d. 644), and more likely dating from

Omar II (d. 720), are little more than Sassanian (Persian) practice which the Arab conquerors took over and adapted to Islamic conditions. This would fit in well with the amply attested fact that the efficient administration of the growing Islamic empire is due to Persian and Byzantine techniques and personnel.

But not only in the sphere of law can we observe this tendency of freeing Islam from Jewish 'influence'. Even in the realm of folklore, a reaction set in against the so-called *Israiliyyat*, stories and legends whose heroes were biblical personalities and whose subjects included pronouncements about the coming of the Messiah, the preceding "birth-pangs" and the "end of days". The edifying value and religious import of these stories should not be underrated, and it was largely for that reason that the prestige which accrued to the Jews was resented.

MONOTHEISM AND UNIVERSALISM

To give substance to this general estimate, we will now discuss at some length and in some detail the affinities between Judaism and Islam and we begin with basic religious beliefs and convictions. Most important of all is the strict uncompromising monotheism preached by Mohammed. "There is no God but Allah"; to impute to Allah companions is crass heresy, an unpardonable sin and crime. Hence the unfaltering opposition to the Christian claim that Jesus was the son of God. But Islam recognised in Jesus a prophet to whom God revealed the gospels, as He revealed the *Torah* to Moses and the *Psalter* to David. God is the creator, the father of mankind.

In the Koran, Mohammed teaches personal responsibility; one of the most important features of the Muslim faith is this insistence on the individual person and his responsibility before God. Originally addressing himself to his fellow-Arabs, Mohammed soon claimed that he was sent by Allah to all mankind. The universalism of Islam has always been one of its greatest glories. It knows no colour bar. (This is, incidentally, one of the strongest reasons why its missionary appeal in Africa and Asia is today so much greater and so much more successful than that of Christianity, apart from dogmatic and doctrinal matters.) Islam does not make great intellectual demands on converts since its creed is simple and direct. The confession "There is no God but Allah and Mohammed is his apostle" opens the door to Islam and full membership of the "community of the faithful" to anybody.

We referred at the beginning of this book to the central position which the Day of Judgment occupies in the Koran. From this concept, there naturally follow the doctrines of Reward and Punishment, of Paradise and Hell and of the Hereafter. Fasting and Repentance and Forgiveness are milestones on the journey of the believer to God. Here is clearly nothing but unequivocal Jewish-Christian heritage, whoever may have transmitted it to Mohammed.

Islam shares with Judaism the belief in a Messiah, called in Arabic '*Mahdi*'. We do not know how far political failure and social injustice have had anything to do with the emergence of the messianic idea in Judaism. In Islam, the Caliph was supreme spiritual guide and political ruler in one. When the Umayyad dynasty wrested power from the family of the Prophet, devout Muslims were deeply disappointed and could not reconcile the rule of the (in their eyes) worldly Umayyads with the ideal demands of Muslim theocracy. Since it was incumbent on every Muslim to obey those in power and authority there was nothing left but to recognise the ruler and even to pray behind him as the Imam, even if he was in theory an unlawful Imam. A *Hadith* explicitly permitted this in order to preserve intact the unity of the community of the faithful. The same idea is expressed in the rabbinic *Avot*: "Do not separate thyself from the congregation".

Though open rebellion was, therefore, ruled out, there was nothing to prevent the faithful hoping for the restoration of the just rule of the four right-guided caliphs. Thus arose the idea of the *Mahdi* whom Allah will send to renew the reign of justice and righteousness on earth. It is chiefly on the point who the *Mahdi* was to be that orthodox or Sunni-Islam is at variance with heterodox or Shi 'i-Islam. The latter, though divided as to the individual member of the family of 'Ali who is to be the *Mahdi*, is united in its allegiance to the house of 'Ali. This is, however, not relevant to our contention that basically the Jewish and the Muslim concept of Messianism is the same. It is immaterial that the Messiah is of the house of David and not a descendant of Moses. What matters is that the ideal is the kingdom of God on earth in justice, righteousness and peace for all mankind united in the belief in the one and only God. This is the common ground both faiths share and their common hope and expectation. It is not impossible that the Jewish idea had something to do with the rise of the Muslim hope. But it is perhaps more likely that it arose independently. The fact remains that in politically troubled times messianic movements sprang to life among Jews no less than among Muslims. Both see in the rule of the divinely revealed law the ideal polity of the future.

While one should not overstress the political aspect, it may yet be stated that no conscientious Jew or Muslim could overlook the gulf that separated the reign of the law from political reality, the ideal life of religion from the actual position. Pietists leave revolution and rebellion to activists and take refuge in messianic hope and expectancy. They sublimate their discontent and horror over a state of affairs so contrary to the revealed will of God, into the patient but fervent longing for the ideal future. In Judaism there was, indeed, more justification for such a hope, since the Messiah is promised in the Bible, and it is no accident that Maimonides made belief in the Messiah one of his thirteen principles of faith. In both faiths this belief and hope enabled the faithful to endure any and every government. It certainly supported the Jews in exile and gave them strength in persecution. Both faiths strongly deprecate any attempt to hasten the coming of the Messiah and to calculate the end-time. But messianic movements have often captured the hearts of the impatient, and calculations of his coming at the end of days are not missing from the pen of Jewish thinkers and leaders of repute, not least in the Muslim period of Jewish history.

BIBLICAL MATERIAL IN THE KORAN

The Koran was brought down from Heaven by the archangel Gabriel; it has its prototype in Heaven as has the *Torah*. It is noteworthy that Mohammed is rather selective in his employment of biblical material. This may be taken as suggesting an initial period of Mohammed's prophetic activity in purely Arab surroundings, a sudden eruption, a genuine religious experience, a spontaneous response to a Divine call. Later, Mohammed related what the Jews told him to his own experience and sought to establish his own prophethood upon the earlier revelation. Consequently, he quotes in the Koran what supports and confirms his message.

He looks upon himself principally as a divinely sent warner, a "clear warner" to his corrupt generation imprisoned in pagan idolatrous worship. Hence he looks for similar warners in the Hebrew Bible and refers, for example,

to Noah in these words (*Sura* xi): "And We sent Noah to
his people: 'I am for you a warner, and a bearer of good
tidings: Serve you none but God. I fear for you the chastise-
ment of a painful day'." (Arberry). Moses, Aaron and
Jonah play a similar role. Typical is *Sura* xxi, entitled *The
Prophets*, where Mohammed proves the revelation of the
one God, His judgment, punishment of evil, reward of
good, and mercy by reference to Moses, Aaron, Abraham,
Lot, Noah, David and Solomon, Job, Ishmael and Idris
(Enoch) in that order, appealing to the believers, as does the
Bible, to *remember* the deeds of God for their own salvation.
There is also an eschatological reference to Gog and Magog,
no doubt a reminiscence of Ezekiel, and, in addition, the
only literal quotation from the Hebrew Bible, Psalms 37. 39
in these words: "For we have written in the Psalms, after
the Remembrance, 'The earth shall be the inheritance of
My righteous servants'. Surely, in this is a Message delivered
unto a people who serve." (Arberry).

Why does Mohammed refer to these biblical personalities
apart from Moses the prophet as prophets? The answer is
that his source was not the Bible but the later *Aggada*, com-
municated to him by word of mouth. It is noteworthy that
Mohammed makes Solomon rectify a wrong judgment of
David and gives him command over the wind, another
example of Midrash. That Solomon should be placed above
David is due to his connection with the Queen of Sheba,
whom according to Muslim tradition, he converted to Islam. As God's messenger he is in a sense a forerunner of
Mohammed.

But of greater significance still is the exceptional position
which Abraham commands in the Koran. This makes him
in one important aspect superior even to Moses. That
Abraham is "the friend" of God goes back to Isaiah (41. 8);
he is neither Jew nor Christian, but, as a true believer in one

God, the first Muslim.* Mohammed's mission is to restore the pure religion of Abraham. This change took place in Medina, and the exaltation of Abraham is the direct result of Mohammed's alienation from the Jews. Of similar significance is the stress laid on Ishmael being the firstborn of Abraham who propagated the *millat Ibrahim*, the religion of Abraham, the "*Imam* of the believers" (*Sura* ii), the founder of the *Ka'bah*, the holy black stone in Mecca.

Mohammed was obviously not able to wean the Arabs from worshipping this stone; in order to give it its legitimate place in Muslim worship, he associated it with Abraham and Ishmael who had settled in Mecca after Abraham had driven out Hagar with his firstborn at the behest of Sarah. The angel Gabriel had saved Hagar and the boy, and the spring of water is sacred to the Muslims as the spring Zemzem. Ishmael married an Arab girl who bore him twelve sons—we think at once of Jacob's twelve sons—and he thus became the ancestor of the northern Arab tribes. The Koran tells the story of Abraham's willingness to sacrifice his—unnamed!—son, and some of the commentators did not hesitate to fill in the name, not of Isaac, but of Ishmael. (At a time when the Persian converts to Islam asserted their rights against the Arabs they claimed descent from Isaac and pointed to him as the son of the free born wife of Abraham to establish their superiority.)

Abraham, as the shining example of unshakeable faith and trust in the one and only God, is flanked in the Koran by Joseph, the *ṣiddīq* (truthful). Mohammed uses the same Arabic root as the Hebrew, meaning 'truth' rather than 'righteousness'. In the Midrash which served him as source for "the fairest of stories", as the Joseph-*Sura* is called, Joseph

---

* A *Muslim* is an adherent of Islam, that is he is one who unquestioningly submits to the will of Allah in complete obedience. A *Mohammedan* is strictly speaking a follower of Mohammed.

is the perfectly righteous person. His steadfastness in the face of temptation is thus overshadowed by his truthfulness in interpreting dreams.

As an illustration of aggadic embellishment a few verses may be quoted. At first Mohammed follows the account in Genesis. But when it comes to the attempt of Potiphar's wife to seduce Joseph the Midrash serves as his pattern: "For she desired him; and he would have taken her, but that he saw the proof of his Lord". The Commentators explain the cryptic "the proof of his Lord" with the help of the *Aggada*, of Midrash and of Talmud, namely, when Joseph wanted to yield to the temptation he saw a vision of his mother, according to some sources, and of his father, according to others, whereupon he conquered his passion. On the other hand, the following incident found its way into the later *Aggada*: "Certain women that were in the city said, 'The Governor's wife has been soliciting her page; he smote her heart with love; we see her in manifest error'. When she heard their sly whispers, she sent to them, and made ready for them a repast, then she gave to each one of them a knife. 'Come forth, attend to them', she said. And when they saw him, they so admired him that they cut their hands, saying, 'God save us! This is no mortal; he is no other but a noble angel'. 'So now you see', she said. 'This is he you blamed me for. Yes, I solicited him, but he abstained. Yet, if he will not do what I command him, he shall be imprisoned, and be one of the humbled' ..." (Arberry)

There are many more aggadic traits in this and in other biblical stories to be found in the Koran. But enough has been quoted to show how much Judaism has contributed to the beliefs of Muslims and to their instruction and edification. But Islam has to some extent repaid its debt; for a number of additions which commentators, biographers of Mohammed and historians have made to the midrashic elements have found their way into the later *Aggada* of medieval Judaism. A large number of midrashic elements are contained in the traditions of Islam known by the term *Ḥadīth*, sayings attributed to Mohammed, stories about his exemplary life and sayings, termed *Sunna*, which will occupy us later. From the *Ḥadīth*, additional material has gone into such works as the *Midrash hagadol*, the *Sepher hayashar*, the *Pirke de R. Eliezer*, the *Shevet Musar*, etc. But these later sources are careful to cleanse the new material of its specifically Islamic import and relevance, for instance, the third visit of Abraham to his son Ishmael during which he consecrated the *Ka'bah* is omitted. On the other hand, Islamic legend attributes many miraculous achievements to Solomon which were accepted into Judaism.

ESCHATOLOGY

Of particular interest is the Jewish element in Muslim eschatological ideas upon which we have already touched in connection with the *Israiliyyat*. Hitherto, it was generally assumed that Christians brought this material to Mohammed and his interpreters, the more so since it stems from apocryphal and apocalyptic texts which are outside the Jewish canon of Scripture, such as the Book of Jubilees and IV Ezra. But since we have found such texts among the Dead Sea Scrolls and such a striking affinity between the Scrolls and this whole literature it is by no means impossible that these writings enjoyed currency among the Jews of Arabia as well. Moreover, a number of descriptions of paradise and hell and of human behaviour when "the hour", "the day of decision" or "resurrection" are approaching can be paralleled from the *Aggada* of the Talmud; thus, man's own limbs testify against him: only a wall separates hell from paradise; the joys of paradise are likened to a banquet. *Sura* lxxiii "If therefore you disbelieve, how will you guard your-selves against a day that shall make the children grey-headed" echoes "And the heads of the children will be white with grey hair" of the *Book of Jubilees*, and *Sura* lxxx "And when the Blast shall sound, upon the day when a man shall flee from his brother, his mother, his father, his consort, his sons ..." (Arberry) is based on the *Ezra Apocalypse*. Similarly, Psalms 49. 8, may have served as the model for *Sura* lxxiv: "Then the intercession of the intercessors shall not profit them", that is, man must face his Judge alone on the Day of Judgment. Again, the idea that man's deeds are entered in a heavenly book which is read out to him on that fearsome day is common to Judaism and Islam.

It has been proposed that the confession of faith "there is no God but Allah" is modelled upon the Aramaic version of II Samuel xxii. 32 and that the koranic designation of God as "sovereign of the worlds" stems from Judaism. Muslim tradition introduces koranic passages with the ex-pression "The Exalted speaks", just as we find biblical quotations in the Talmud preceded by "The Merciful (*Rachmana*) speaks".

BIBLICAL HISTORY

Before taking our leave of the Bible, we must observe that commentators, and especially Muslim historians, have incorporated biblical history into their narrative for two reasons. In the first place, biblical history proves the mani-festation of God in history and it, moreover, legitimises Mohammed's revelation which is thus linked with the be-ginning of history, with the very creation of the world and man as the servant of God. Islam has thus entered into the inheritance of the Jews; its own history is the legitimate succession to that of the people of Israel. There is thus not only historical continuity but also an unbroken *Heilsgeschichte*, salvation being the goal of mankind. Another interesting corollary of this appropriation of biblical history is this: In the controversy whether the Caliphate was a divinely ordained or a human institution the theologians and jurists appealed to the Koran. God says in *Sura* ii: "I am setting in the earth a viceroy" and in *Sura* xxxviii the caliph's duty to act as a judge is stated in these words: " 'David, behold, We have appointed thee a viceroy in the earth; therefore judge between men justly, and follow not caprice, lest it lead thee astray from the way of God …' ". The kingdom belongs to God, as in Judaism.

The other reason for including biblical history is, though in a different way, no less significant. The Arabs are very proud of their descent and attach great importance to genealogy. Their nobility is greatly enhanced by their ability to trace their ancestry to the patriarchs whom they looked upon as prophets of God, in particular to Abraham, the first Muslim, the father of Ishmael the progenitor of the Arab tribes, as stated earlier. Ibn Khaldūn, the famous 14th century Muslim philosopher of history, devoted considerable space to biblical history. In this he followed the tradition of Muslim historiography, but went further than his sources by extending his account to the Second Commonwealth, making full use of Josippon.

FALSIFICATION OF SCRIPTURE

A final point: acquaintance with the Jewish sources through Jews, Jewish converts, commentators and collectors of *Ḥadīth* underlined many discrepancies and contradictions between Mohammed's Koran and the Bible. Undoubtedly, this played a considerable part from the beginning in stiffening Arab and particularly Jewish opposition to Mohammed, and it was therefore imperative to safeguard the divine character of the Koran and the correctness of tradition; hence, the Muslim claim, already made once by the Christians, that the Jews had deliberately falsified their Scriptures. The Muslim presentation was the correct one, it reflected the true wording and meaning of the Hebrew Scriptures which had been tampered with by the Jews for polemical reasons. This confirmed the Koran and added lustre to its author, the seal of the prophets, sent by Allah with the final revelation in clear Arabic.

CULT AND RITUAL

The inclusion in Koran and *Hadīth* of fundamental religious ideas and concepts and of the men who personify them in the Hebrew Bible and the *Aggada* of rabbinic Judaism is clear evidence of the impact of Judaism on Islam. Equally close affinity can be observed in the realm of religious duties in the narrower sense, that is, in cult and ritual, as well as in important branches of law, especially personal status law, and in jurisprudence. This is to be expected since both Islam and Judaism are based upon and centred in a book which lays down the duties between man and God and between man and man. We will briefly discuss some of the more striking affinities in cultic duties.

Islam knows, just like Judaism, the distinction between clean and unclean and lays down in similar detail what defiles and how to regain ritual purity by ablutions and immersion. In principle the laws governing *taharah* are the same, as is the term itself. They concern forbidden food and drink, touching the private parts, discharge, contact with a corpse or a carcass, all of which cause ritual impurity and bar the affected from fulfilling such religious duties as prayer, presence in the mosque and reciting the Koran. Unlike Judaism, Islam does not demand such sacrifices as are decreed in Leviticus, nor does it set a time limit before purity can be regained; it simply requires ablutions or immersion in accordance with the degree of defilement.

PRAYER

Although *taharah* comes first in time as a necessary prerequisite, the foremost religious duty of a Muslim is prayer, *salāt*. It is difficult to decide whether the five daily prayers go back to the five prayers on the Day of Atonement or strike the mean between Jewish and Christian practice. We know from the *Hadīth* that during his ascension to heaven Mohammed was at first commanded to institute fifty daily prayers, but had them eventually reduced to five through the repeated intercession of Moses. (One thinks of the intercession of Abraham for Sodom and Gomorrah.)

The first essential in prayer is *nīya*, intention, exactly corresponding to the Jewish *kavanah* (*Mishnah Berachot*). Without it prayer is useless. Next in importance is the direction in prayer, *qibla*. In his Meccan period, Mohammed fixed the direction to Jerusalem; in Medina, after he had fallen out with the Jews, he changed it to Mecca. As the day for public prayer, *salāt al-jum'a*, Mohammed fixed Friday, the day on which the Jews prepared for their Sabbath, and he declared specifically that it was not to be a day of rest like the Jewish Sabbath and the Christian Sunday. This is ostentatiously directed against "the people of the book". That *taharah* and *nīya* are imitations of the conditions for

Jewish prayer as laid down in *Mishnah* and *Gemara Berachot* is fairly obvious. Apparently, the Jews of northern Arabia observed these conditions strictly in Mohammed's time. The same may well be true of the frequent kneelings and prostrations prescribed for Muslim prayer, although this is usually associated with the monastic Christian practice. That the term *ṣalāt* is derived from the Aramaic *tselotha* does not prove a Christian origin any more than a Jewish one, since, as has been stated before, both used Aramaic. However, the scales are probably weighted in favour of a Jewish model since Professor Mittwoch has established that it corresponds to the *tephillah* in its precise meaning of *amida* (or the "eighteen benedictions" said standing) which has also to be said standing. He finds traces of the *amida* in the Muslim formula "Allah is great" since the first of the "eighteen benedictions" includes the phrase *ha'el hag-gadol*. Moreover, the second important element of the *tephillah*, namely the *Shema*, is represented in the *ṣalāt* through the recital of the opening *Sura* of the Koran which is known by the technical term *qira'a*. Likewise, the recital of the *Salām* (peace) corresponds to the last benediction, the *birkat hashalom*.

Whether the *minbar* has as its pattern the *bima* (*almemar*) of the Synagogue or the pulpit of the church is also difficult to determine. But in any case, the *minbar* was used for the delivery of the *ḥutbah* (sermon) by the *Imam* who corresponds to the *sheliach tsibbur*, the leader of the congregation in prayer. The two parts of the *ḥutbah* may be identical with the reading of *Torah* and *Haftarah*, unless they are modelled upon the Christian reading from Scripture and sermon. It is uncertain whether the Christian custom goes back to Judaism or not. The *mu'adhdhin* calls the faithful to prayer from the minaret of the mosque, as is well known. The first call (*adhān*) from the minaret is followed by a second call in the mosque. Mittwoch thinks the second *adhān* is reminiscent of the invitation to prayer with the following recital of the *Shema* by the *Chazan* of the Synagogue. Communal prayer is meritorious in Islam as in Judaism; but Islam does not stipulate a *minyan*, a quorum of worshippers. Muslims are to appear in festive attire in the mosque on Friday, just like the Jews on the Sabbath. Friday must not be observed as a fastday, just like Sabbath (except that the Day of Atonement can fall on a Sabbath). Just as the Midrash tells us that the fire of hell does not burn on the Sabbath, so it does not burn on a Friday in Islam. It may be added that Islam likewise knows of special prayers, such as those for rain, in illness, on a voyage, etc.

It is interesting to see Islamic influence in this sphere at a later date. Abraham Maimuni, son and successor of Maimonides as *Nagid* of Egyptian Jewry, introduced—one might say more correctly, re-introduced—prostrations into the synagogue service, following the Muslim custom. He also wanted the congregation to face the Ark in prayer, sitting upright like the Muslims. These innovations roused considerable opposition and led to a complaint to the Sultan against the *Nagid* who hastened to assure the Muslim ruler that this was his private arrangement which need not be imitated by those who objected. (Goitein)

DIETARY LAWS

In connection with *tahara*, defilement through forbidden food was mentioned. Mohammed came to reject most of the dietary laws, which he considered a punishment for the Jews. But he retained the prohibition on eating pig, blood and carcasses and decreed ritual slaughtering of all animals permitted for human consumption. Muslim slaughtering corresponds exactly to Jewish *Shechitah* and at first Mohammed insisted that it should be accompanied by the recital of benedictions. Gradually this "burden of the Law" was lightened until nothing but *Shechitah* was retained since a Muslim always conscious of the presence of Allah had no need even to mention the name of God. As is well known, however, Judaism also knows of lenient application of the law, as, for instance, if a person cannot say the prescribed prayers in the synagogue, or in his house, or in the field, or even on his bed, he should at least think of God.

FASTING

The next basic religious duty of a Muslim is fasting. Originally, Mohammed instituted the so-called *'Ashura* fast on the Jewish Day of Atonement, that is, as its name also used by Aramaic-speaking Jews, implies on the tenth day. According to a *Ḥadīth*, his attention was drawn to the fact that the Jews observed the tenth day of Tishri as their *'Ashura* fast, whereupon Mohammed fixed the ninth day for it. But others wanted to fast on the eleventh day as well, so finally a whole month, the *Ramadhan*, was set aside for fasting. But only from sunrise to sunset were Muslims to fast, and they were enjoined not to prolong the fast as the Jews did, but to break it in haste. They were allowed to eat and drink—but no wine, which was totally forbidden,—until dawn when they can distinguish the white from the black thread of daybreak (a phrase reminiscent of *Talmud Berachot*). Deliberate deviations emphasise Jewish origin no less than do similarities. Thus, imitation exists side by side with opposition, as can be seen in the remarkable parallel between the Muslim and the Jewish fast. Jewish tradition connects *Yom Kippur* with the giving of the second Tables of the Law by God to Moses on Sinai, and Muslim tradition makes the *tanzīl*, the sending down of the Koran from Heaven through Gabriel to Mohammed, take place on the *'Ashura* fast.

Another example of a change from strict observance of a Jewish custom to a relaxation can be seen in the lenient interpretation of one of the koranic commands. This demands the recital of a benediction before eating, but it was later interpreted, on the basis of the verbal form used, to be desirable but not obligatory. Thus, a necessary act became merely a meritorious one.

The fourth basic religious duty of the Muslim is the *Hajj*, the pilgrimage to Mecca. Every Muslim is enjoined to undertake this pilgrimage at least once during his lifetime if he is able to afford it. The principal ceremony of the *Hajj* consists of making a circuit of the black stone, the *Ka'bah*, seven times. Once the *Ka'bah* was turned into a Muslim sanctuary it was natural to institute a pilgrimage to it, the more so since Mohammed had changed the direction in prayer from Jerusalem to the *Ka'bah* in Mecca.

SOCIAL DUTIES

In Islam, as in Judaism, every duty and obligation, even what normally falls under ordinary private and public law, is considered a religious duty incumbent upon every believer and ultimately due to God. The religious duties so far dealt with are all personal duties which the individual owes to God. The last of these duties, the poor-tax (*zakāt*), the fifth pillar of Islam, is a social duty and recognises social justice as a fundamental religious commandment. It roughly corresponds to *tsedakah* in Judaism, which designation is used as a synonym of *zakāt*. It is to be paid into a separate finance department, called *bait mal Allah*, the treasury of God, in contradistinction from the treasury of the State, called *bait mal al-muslimin*, treasury of the Muslims. It is the only tax imposed on the Muslims, all normal taxation, that is the poll- and land-taxes discussed earlier, falls upon the *dhimmis* as "people of the book". In application it is a kind of tithe (*ma'aser*); indeed, ten per cent is due on produce from grain, date palms and fruit trees; on domestic animals and on silver and gold only two and a half per cent. Although it is called poor-tax, its yield is not used solely for the poor, but also, for instance, for impecunious strangers and for slaves who wish to redeem themselves.

The care of widows and orphans is likewise a religious duty, and visiting the sick is commended. The *Hadīth* reads: "Accompany the dead [to their rest], visit the sick and spread peace"; this is no doubt taken from the saying in *Mishnah Pea*. Many more parallels with aggadic recommendations for mercy and compassion, stressing social justice and, in general, ethical behaviour can be gleaned from the vast *Hadīth* literature, among them Hillel's golden rule. In the Muslim version, the heathen, in order to enter paradise, is enjoined to fulfil the Muslim duties and in addition to give to others what he would wish to receive and to spare them what he himself does not like. The essentially religious motivation of these social duties is apparent from another tradition which has its origin in *Talmud Berachot*; this says that when God had completed the creation He wrote into His book over the throne: "My mercy has vanquished my wrath".

SPECIFIC LAWS

Turning to similarities in specific laws, only a few illustrations can be given. Although some branches of law have received comparative treatment, much detailed research by scholars equally versed in Jewish and Muslim law is needed before a clear picture emerges on which a comprehensive exposition can be built.

Owing to the origin and development of Islam as an expansionist movement the basis of its law is really a law of war. Islam divided the world into a realm of Islam and a realm of war. The non-Muslim peoples are to be subjected to *jihād*, holy war, and are to be reduced and ultimately to be absorbed into the realm of Islam. It was, therefore, a condition of war which frequently determined the formulation of Muslim law. Hence, the first concern for the Muslim was the determination of his share in booty, the rights and duties of the protected "people of the book", rules of warfare and treatment of prisoners of war. In this connection it is interesting to note that the law governing female prisoners is identical with that laid down in Deuteronomy 21. The restrictions imposed on *dhimmis* were mentioned earlier on. Here, we would only add that although they were protected, their position in law is inferior in that no Jew or other *dhimmi* can testify against a Muslim in a court of law.

Further, although Islam knows the *ius talionis*, it allows blood money to be substituted for the death penalty. In the case of a Jew being killed, *talio* is not permissible, but only blood money amounting to a third of the value. If the victim is a Muslim, blood money to the full value is exacted. We note the basic agreement between Judaism and Islam in the substitution of *mamon* for *mamash*.

One instance at least from commercial law may be quoted: Islam forbids usury and the taking of interest, as Judaism does.

Lastly, an example of Jewish parallelism if not direct influence from the sphere of private or personal status law.

Mohammed is rightly credited with a beneficial reform of
the marriage laws and with the betterment of the position
of woman. There is a definite connection between Muslim
and Jewish laws of marriage and divorce. The husband has
to make a marriage contract with his wife and to write
a dowry into the marriage settlement. The term *mahr* is the
same as the biblical *mohar*. Two witnesses are needed at the
conclusion of the contract. A Muslim's wives all have equal
rights. The principal grounds for a divorce are the same in
both religions; the actual divorce in Islam can be effected by
a judge who can act at the instance of the wife as well as
of the husband provided sufficient grounds exist; or by the
husband; or by agreement between the partners. In detail,
however, there are considerable differences between Jewish
and Muslim law, as, for instance, in the question of polygamy
which rabbinic law forbids while Mohammedan law per-
mits a man to marry up to four wives. In the matter of
re-marriage, Islam is more lenient. Mohammed's regulations concerning forbidden marriages correspond very
closely to the relevant Jewish stipulations, except that he
prohibits marriage between uncle and niece, as do the
Karaites and other Jewish sects.

At first he adopted the same penalty for adultery as
biblical law, namely death by stoning, but he later reduced
it to stripes. One of the four recognised rites, that of
Al-Shafi 'i, demands four witnesses whereas Jewish Law
requires only two. The wording of the specific question the
witnesses must be able to answer in the affirmative is the
same as that employed in *Talmud Makkot*. Again, the laws
of *niddah*, relating to the menstruous woman, also apply in
Islam, but they are less rigid: another example of acceptance
in principle, but of a relaxation in practice.

Many more examples could be adduced to show the
presence of Jewish legal material in Muslim law in all its

branches. What has been discussed so far must, however, suffice to show that in the realm of *Halachah* no less than in that of *Aggada* Islam is indebted to Judaism, be it by way of complete or partial acceptance, modification or outright rejection and opposition.

JURISPRUDENCE

It may be useful, therefore, to turn from practice to theory and to compare the concept of law in both systems, its character, its principles and methods. Such a treatment will not only bring out essential similarities, but will also teach us to beware of rash generalisations and of the too ready assumption of influence when a parallel development may be all we can safely deduce. For from the outset we must realise that Islam as a Semitic religion may have arrived at its concept of the perfect unalterable catholic law without consciously modelling itself on the monotheistic faiths among which it arose, in particular on Judaism with its all-embracing *Torah*.

Naturally, every religion which claims that its law is a revelation from God must attempt to develop and consolidate this law if it wants to maintain its sole authority over its adherents. In a society like the Muslim, which is composed of so many ethnic groups with diverse aspirations and social and cultural standards, such a religion can and does serve as a unifying bond and focal point only if its law controls both the temporal and spiritual realms. In fact, Islam is not a Church and the caliph is not a pope. The caliph is charged as the "Commander of the Faithful" and Imam with military leadership, and as judge with the maintenance of law and order and the defence of Islam with the aid of the divine law. This is at least the constitutional theory of Islam even though the Islamic State in practice has fallen short of the ideal. The claim of the *Sharī'a* or divinely revealed law of Islam has never been set aside, though its demands have had to take second place behind the exigencies of political life most of the time. The State was only entitled to legislate in the field of military and civil administration, and the Head of State was anxious to obtain the sanction of the jurists for his enactments.

We might call this claim of the sovereignty of the *Sharī'a* and of its unquestioned authority a fiction; the fact is that this fiction outlived the life of the caliphate and proved strong enough to maintain Islam to our own day. The postulated unity of 'religion' and 'politics' has presented Islam with baffling practical and theoretical problems which have caused severe stress and strain and tested the ingenuity of its spiritual leaders to such an extent that the Islamic character of the modern Arab States is uncertain even where Islam is the state religion. This is, naturally, nothing new; it began with the Umayyads and continued through the rule of the Abbasids and in the successor states. The difference between then and now is only that the religious basis and centre of life has been seriously questioned with the emergence of the modern national state and its westernising tendencies with the result that the reality of the theoretical rule of the religious all-embracing law is either gone or at least is seriously threatened in many parts of Asia and Africa where Islam is practised. State and religion are no longer co-terminous, neither in theory nor in actual fact.

THE CONCEPT OF LAW

But let us return to the time of Islam's emergence and to the establishment of its law spanning every manifestation of

individual and social life. The resemblance between the
Shari'a and the *Torah* is striking in their identical
claim to the complete allegiance of their peoples. Obviously, the practical application of this claim must needs
differ in the two communities since the Muslim community
led a full political existence with a government and administration responsible for internal security and defence
against enemies and charged with the propagation of the
faith. The *Torah* could operate only within the religious,
social and cultural autonomy granted to the Jewish minority.
In fact, 'religious' was and is as comprehensive in meaning
and extent in Judaism as in Islam. But Judaism was spared
the inevitable conflict between the religious ideal demand
and political aspirations which have their own impetus and
create their own laws and standards. This is notwithstanding
the fact that the Jewish law, the *Halachah* a product of the
Galut, claims to legislate for an independent sovereign
Jewish State as much as Islam does. The *Halachah* was developed in a political vacuum so-to-speak, that is by devout
Jews without political responsibility, whose ideal norms
could not be tested in the crucible of a normal State-life. Is
not the problem of 'religion' in the State of Israel clear proof
of this? We shall see later how Judaism did not only give to
Islam, but was also enriched by it, though more in form
than in substance.

We might, perhaps, benefit from studying the history of
the *Shari'a* in Islam. We might perchance learn how to
adapt and reactivate the *Halachah* to the needs of a modern
sovereign national state by reminding ourselves and the
Muslims of the common ground of law. The alternatives
are surely the same for Jewish Israelis and for Muslim Arabs:
a religious law capable of meeting the needs of a modern
tate by giving its political direction a spiritual driving
power based on fundamental Jewish or Muslim tenets and

social and ethical ideas and institutions, or a secular state
built on the rule of law as understood in a democratic
society with freedom of religion. In the latter case, religion
will become the private concern of the individual citizen,
even if Judaism and Islam were to be the religion of the
respective states. In such a state, both religions would become a church, something neither Judaism nor Islam can
ever be by definition. The unity of 'religion' and 'politics'
would have to be abandoned even as an ideal, and the
separation of church and state would have to be acknowledged in theory as well as in practice. I am not speaking of
Judaism in the *Galut*, nor would I claim that, logical as the
stated alternatives may seem for Israel and the Arab States,
such a separation would be a solution, let alone the only
solution. I merely submit that such an alternative appears to
be a plausible deduction from a consideration of the
character and meaning of an all-embracing religious law as
represented by the *Torah* and the *Shari'a*, whose claim and
binding force are no longer generally recognised.

REVELATION

Such a consideration may now be briefly attempted: the
fundamental axiom is that of Divine revelation, which
means that the primary source and fountainhead of all law
is the written *Torah* in Judaism and the Koran in Islam.
Neither are law books, and although the *Torah* contains
many more "laws, statutes and ordinances" in legal form
than does the Koran both revelations contain primarily
beliefs and ethical maxims which must guide their believers.
This means two things: the ethical basis for the good life
(wherein 'good' means an absolute value because it comes
from God, the all-knowing personal God, the source and

embodiment of ethics); and the ethical purpose of law in all its branches, contained both explicitly and implicitly in the Book. Both contain theocratic law which has its source in the sovereign will of God, the God of justice and mercy. Both legislate for a community of brothers.

For the reader who is not familiar with Islam, two quotations from the Koran may demonstrate this: "We have set thee upon a Highway (*Sharī'a*) of Command, do thou therefore follow it" (*Sura* xlv) and: "The believers indeed are brothers; so set things right between your two brothers, and fear God; haply so you will find mercy" (*Sura* xlix). Significantly, the first quotation is preceded by a statement which shows the importance of Judaism for Mohammed and explains why he was sent with his own book. It reads thus: "Indeed, We gave the Children of Israel the Book, the Judgment, and the Prophethood, and We provided them with good things, and We preferred them above all beings. We gave them clear signs of the Command; so they differed not, except after the knowledge had come to them, being insolent one to another. Surely thy Lord will decide between them on the Day of Resurrection touching their differences." (Arberry)

Prof. H. A. R. Gibb aptly says: "Law is the external aspect of religion; that is to say, it is the attempt to give formal shape and definition to the multiple relations existing between man and God, and man and man." He supports this definition by a quotation from a Muslim jurist: "The science of Law is the knowledge of the rights and duties whereby man is enabled to observe right conduct in this life, and to prepare himself for the world to come." The Rabbis have divided law into laws regulating the relations between man and God and those regulating the relations between man and man. Precisely because the Book was revealed at a certain juncture in the life of a people the law

derived from it had to be kept flexible to meet new conditions. This applies to Islam even more than to Judaism for,
as stated earlier, Islam expanded and incorporated peoples
with laws and customs of their own. To secure unity these
local customs had to be brought into line with the revealed
law. How was this to be effected? In the first place the range
of revelation had to be extended.

ORAL LAW

This was achieved in Judaism by adding the oral tradition
to the written *Torah* and by claiming that the oral tradition
originated with Moses on Sinai (*Halachah leMoshe miSinai*).
Halachah has the same meaning as *Sharī'a*, 'the Highway' of
the Koran, the straight road leading to God. In Islam the
second root is likewise tradition, the tradition of Mohammed's *Sunna* or exemplary life and sayings to guide his
community, collected in the *Hadīth* of which there exist six
authoritative collections, two of which are termed 'sound'.
Their authentic character is established by an unbroken
chain of trustworthy tradition going back to the Prophet or
one of his companions. The technical term is *isnād* which has
its counterpart in Judaism, for example in *Avot*, the chain
of Tradition is traced from Moses to the Men of the Great
Synagogue and in many passages in the Talmud where
decisions and interpretations are given in the name of one
or more Rabbis. *Halachah* is thus the decision of a majority
of rabbis or of one whose authority is recognised by that
majority, the *Chachamim*. Much of the Oral *Torah* is custom
to which the application of *Halachah leMoshe miSinai* lent
both the antiquity and authority required to attain the status
and force of law. It will be necessary to enlarge on the importance of custom in Jewish and Muslim law a little later.

First, we must round off the constituent sources of law.

With the growth of the Islamic empire, the Muslim jurists found that Koran and *Sunna* were not sufficient to frame new laws to meet new needs. They, therefore, added two further roots: *qiyās*, analogy, combined with *ra'y*, (personal) opinion. In this way, laws could be deduced from the two primary 'roots', Koran and *Sunna*, by means of analogy and inference, assisted by the logical discernment, *ra'y*, of the doctors of the law. The subjective element involved was checked by the all-important fourth 'root' *ijmā'*, consensus, that is, the agreement of the Muslim community represented by the scholars, *'ulama*, of the age. It will be obvious that *qiyās* has its counterpart in Judaism in the exegetical rule (*midda*) of *hekkesh* or perhaps rather of *kal vechomer*, while *ijmā'* corresponds to the decision arrived at by the majority of scholars, the *Chachamim*, or their concurrence with the view of one among them whose authority they recognised.

Other corresponding rules of interpretation may be discovered upon further investigation; that some go back to Roman law has been asserted by some scholars but denied by others. It is a problem which we face in Jewish jurisprudence as well. But the opinion may be ventured that the character of both Jewish and Muslim law with their basis in revelation makes a conscious and deliberate borrowing from an entirely different system not very likely. It is, thus, more likely that the terms *'ulama* or *fuqaha* for the Muslim jurists correspond rather to the *Chachamim* than to the Roman *prudentes*. In any case *'ulama* is in etymology and meaning so much nearer to *Chachamim* that the connection with Jewish law appears more plausible. After all *chochmah* means the wisdom of *Torah*, and we need only remember that Iraq as the centre of halachic activity provided the meeting ground of Muslim jurists in the formative period of the

Sharī'a with learned Jews among whom a number were
converts, as stated earlier, who brought their knowledge of
Jewish law and its methods and principles to bear on the
nascent Muslim law. The synonym *fuqaha* for *'ulama* derives
from *Fiqh*, the term for the science of law in Islam. *Fiqh*, as
the science of the *Sharī'a*, is sometimes used as its synonym.
We might thus say that, broadly conceived, Written plus
Oral Law equals *Sharī'a*, and *Halachah* equals *Fiqh*.

The similarities between the Muslim 'roots' (*usūl*) and
the Jewish *middot* as such, and to some extent at least also in
detail, are obvious, but there are some important divergences. Thus, *Sunna* is much more closely bound up with
Mohammed than Oral tradition in Judaism is with the actual
life and thought expressed in 'traditions' of Moses. The
principle is the same, naturally. The *Halachah* is theoretically
led back to Moses's sinaitic revelation; but it is simply stated
as a principle, an axiomatic assumption to legitimise the
authority of the rabbis' legislative activity. In Islam, the
"chain of tradition" must start with Mohammed or one of
his companions who vouch for its authenticity and its having
originated with Mohammed. Nor is the agreement of the
experts identical in both systems. *Ijmā'* is irrevocable; once
a decision has been reached by *ijmā'* it cannot be set aside.
Discussion cannot be reopened. This is established by the
saying attributed to Mohammed: "my community will
never agree upon an error". There is no such claim to
infallibility in Judaism. We have seen that, in Islam, the
"agreement of the community" is in fact the "agreement of
those who have power to bind and to loosen", that is, the
'ulama. This claim has had the important effect that *ijmā'*
became almost as powerful an element in shaping *Fiqh* as the
two primary "roots" of divine inspiration, Koran and
Sunna. For nothing could become *Sunna* that was not
sanctioned by *ijmā'* as much, if not actually more, than

by the unbroken chain of tradition, an external criterion.

The infallibility of *ijmā'* is due to the fact that it is to be considered the result of inspiration. For Mohammed is said to have stated: "The wise (*'ulama*) of my community are like the prophets of the people of Israel", and another *Ḥadīth*— in imitation of the talmudic saying "prophecy was taken away from the prophets and given to the wise (*chachamim*)" —states: "the wise (or scholars, *'ulama*) are the heirs of the prophets". In view of this unmistakable dependence on Judaism it is the more striking that Islam should have made *ijmā'* irrevocable. It is another indication of the independent handling of borrowed material.

Connected with this infallibility is another trait of Muslim law which distinguishes *Fiqh* from *Halachah*: the flexibility of Jewish law was guaranteed and its rigours eased by the method adopted by the rabbis in the *Gemara* of giving the whole discussion leading to the decision. Not only is the minority view recorded, but the possibility of reopening the discussion and of solving new problems with the help of the talmudic discussion was given. This enabled later genera-tions to make necessary adjustments and to maintain the universal validity of the *Halachah* by adding decisions and enactments in the spirit though not in the letter of the re-vealed Law. Moreover, they were helped in their task of interpreting the Law authoritatively and of making new decisions as the need arose by being in touch with the people at large. This contact was maintained by the commandment of *Talmud Torah*, or study of the Law which is incumbent upon every Jew. The Muslim jurists were much more a class apart and much more isolated in that knowledge of *Fiqh* was much more confined to the experts in Islam. However, in both religions, the principle was established that no ordin-ance could be enforced unless the majority could bear it (*Talmud Bava Batra*). In Islam a tradition says: "Allah lays upon each man only what he can fulfil". Incidentally, this saying shows clearly how Islam, though upholding the concept of the community, is really concerned about the individual Muslim in the first place, much more so than Judaism, which sees in the individual primarily a member of the community, of the people of Israel.

LAW AND CUSTOM

We know that the rabbis were aware of the changing situation and the Jewish position within another society and that they made allowance for "the needs of the times" and realised the necessity of "the adjustment of human relations". New rules and regulations for the sake of social peace and good-neighbourly relations—notwithstanding hostility, open or concealed, and even persecution—were made throughout the Middle Ages under Muslim and Christian rule. The rabbis based their decisions on the principle acknowledged in the Talmud in statements like: "custom annuls law", "custom always precedes law" and "everything depends upon local custom". The Talmud and its authority had to be maintained intact and valid; but at the same time local custom could not be ignored except to the detriment of the contemporary generation of Jews who recognised the authority of the Talmud, yet had to adjust their lives, that is in the first place their livelihood, to their surroundings. The conflict between talmudic law and custom was rarely solved except by recourse to casuistry. But the overriding authority of the Talmud was never doubted. Custom was recognised in practice and the Talmud, while retaining its valid, immutable authority, was temporarily ignored, but not abrogated.

In Islam, we meet with a similar development and attitude

in principle. It seems more likely that similar circumstances led to similar measures and results independently from Judaism. We need hardly stress that the actual situation was different. For the Jews were a tolerated minority and the Muslims the ruling majority. Moreover, the Jews had to abide by the ruling that *dina demalchuta dina*, that is, that the civil law of the government superseded the Jewish civil law, which put a different complexion upon Jewish practice altogether.

In Islam, flexibility was achieved by the axiom (to quote H. A. R. Gibb): "the general rule is permissibility". It applied, however, only to what was not expressly prescribed or forbidden. But it enabled the jurists to reach a decision in accordance with the requirements of the case in question, based on the *ijmā*, and thus obtaining binding legal force. Not all jurists in all parts of the empire at all times arrived at the same decisions. Hence, 'schools' or 'rites' arose, of which four were eventually accepted as equally orthodox. We might think of a similar though less rigid and formalised arrangement in Judaism: the schools of Hillel and Shammai. The resemblance does not go very far, for with the exception of six cases where the decision was not according to the view of either of them and of three according to the school of Shammai, the universally accepted decision as agreed upon in the *Gemara* followed the school of Hillel. In Islam, uniformity is not so close and complete, but divergences between one or more of the four schools are confined to minor details.

It has often been said that Islam makes more allowance for human weakness than Judaism does in matters of law. This is undoubtedly so. What matters is, in fact, that the law framers in both systems were anxious to arrive at their decisions after full consideration of the human element, as is clear from the above quotation about the majority in both laws. Just as Islam as a whole is something in its own right despite its borrowings from Judaism and Christianity, so is Muslim law, despite all affinities with Jewish law, anything but a copy. We spoke in the beginning of the genius of Mohammed and of his being rooted in Arabia and its people. The same ability to imprint on foreign ideas and institutions the indigenous attitudes and ways which we encounter in religious ideas and institutions we also meet in the domain of law. This alone sufficed to give the religious law of Islam its peculiar stamp, its Arab character, which is less apparent in detail—here 'influence' is evident—than in general; and therefore it is difficult to pin down and isolate. It is, to follow Prof. Gibb once more, the principle of *inṣāf*, which roughly corresponds to some extent to the concept of equity. Its intention is to produce an equitable settlement of conflict between parties and claims. "To give every man his due" is the basic principle of Bedouin justice and ... it is explicitly taken up and made mandatory in the Koranic text: "Bring about a reconciliation between your two brothers". Prof. Gibb rightly stresses the modification of Arabian customs in Islam and applies it to *inṣāf* in relation to the Divine law thus: "in theory, the Divine Law supplied a solution for every case, but its solutions were 'type' solutions which had in practice to be applied to specific cases by adopting the principles of *inṣāf*. Thus its impersonal precepts were brought into harmony with the intensely personal conception of justice to which the Eastern peoples have always clung". I am not aware of an exact equivalent of *inṣāf* in Jewish law. But in principle the same attitude is prevalent in Judaism, as has been shown in connection with law and custom and the principles that govern their relationship. I would again stress the difference: Judaism had not only to cope with its own adherents and to take account of the human factor in its own house, but it had also to contend with the outside world; Jewish life was largely determined by the facts of *Galut*.

It is the more interesting to observe the method adopted in Islam to deal with what we encountered in Judaism as "local custom". Owing to its origin and development, as has been so often stated, Islam burst into existing civilisations with their own laws and customs. These were termed by the Muslim jurists *'ada* (custom) or *'urf* (what is done). Although not on the same level with the *Sharī'a*, it could not be ignored as it was deeply rooted in the people who lived by it. Naturally, many such customs did not run counter to the ideal *Sharī'a* and did not have to be accommodated to it. But there were customs which could not be squared with the *Sharī'a* any more than could certain customs with the *Halachah*. Hence there was a continuous process of gradual accommodation and modification. In both systems this procedure was only possible because each had a high sense of responsibility to the ideal divinely revealed law and was imbued with a humane feeling of fairness and equity. Jurists in both systems strove sincerely and persistently to let justice prevail in the inevitable clash between absolute justice stemming from God—as they understood it—and human custom.

JUDGES AND JURISTS

Justice was administered in Islam by judges, called *qadi*. Each of the four orthodox rites had its own judges. In addition, it entrusted the task of regulating the relationship between specific practical cases and the ideal *Sharī'a* to a special category of jurists, the *muftis*. They consider the circumstances and situations of a practical legal problem, look for precedents and study the *Sharī'a* for guidance. The result is a decision, called *fatwa*. These *fatwas* possessed binding legal force. We shall see later how the legal activity of the Geonim in Babylonia was influenced by this practice.

While the *dayan* would correspond to the *qadi*, there is no equivalent to the *mufti* in Judaism. Every ordained rabbi who has obtained *Semichah* has the power to decide questions of law in Judaism. This is another instance of how the knowledge of *Halachah* and the ability to interpret it authoritatively is much more widespread in Judaism simply because study is a general commandment and learning is not confined to a professional class. However, the jurists proper in the post-talmudic ages have gradually developed into a profession as well, and when we compare the professional jurists in Judaism and Islam we can discern an interesting parallel development. Expertise in authoritative interpretation and in framing legal decisions is confined to a limited number of professional jurists as distinct from learned laymen, that is those who can 'lernen' Talmud, whose numbers no doubt varied from time to time in Judaism, but who are absent in Islam.

The parallel between Judaism and Islam consists in the clear distinction in both systems between generations of jurists. In both there exists the same gulf between the creative lawyers of the formative period of the religious law and the guardians of tradition who foreswear all independence and lean on the authority of their predecessors.

In Judaism we have the *Tannaim* who devised the rules of interpretation and applied them to the *Torah* using their independent judgment. By discussion with like-minded, equally qualified colleagues and sustained argument they arrived at the *Halachah*. They were succeeded by the *Amoraim* who formed the middle generation between the *Tannaim*, the scholars of the Mishna, and the later *Saboraim* and geonim who cover the period from the completion of the Talmud to the middle of the tenth century. The two latter groups no longer decided legal problems independently, but based themselves on the previous generations: the *Amoraim* based themselves on the Mishna and Baraita, that is on the collected and fixed oral tradition which they considered as the authority by which they felt bound in their own decisions. But within these limits they showed great flexibility and ingenuity and in the end produced the Talmud which, in turn, became the authority for the following generations of halachists. Both groups neither possessed nor claimed equal authority with their predecessors, but to them we owe the continued growth, development and flexibility of the *Halachah*.

In Islam, a similar development took place. The creative jurists who framed and developed the *Fiqh* or *Sharī'a* practised independent judgment (*ijtihād*) and are therefore called *mujtahids*. This process of legal formulation occupied the first two centuries of Islam, whereas from the third century onwards the Muslim jurists practised *taqlīd*, that is, they relied on the decisions of the *mujtahids*, derived their own decisions from them and 'clothed' them with the authority of their predecessors. They are, therefore, known as *muqallids*. They neither possessed nor claimed the authority to make independent decisions; all they were prepared to do was to base their own decisions on existing law. It is a recurring feature of legal history in Islam that, especially in periods of stress and strain between the authority of the law and the political authority of the government, jurists and theologians appealed for the reopening of *ijtihād*, of independent judgment, in order to restore the effective authority of the *Sharī'a*. One of the outstanding features of modernism in Islam is—at any rate for the traditionalists among its champions—the insistent call for a re-interpretation and re-activation of *Fiqh* through the courageous and consistent exercise of *ijtihād*. If a non-Muslim may be allowed to venture an opinion it seems indeed imperative that this method should be vigorously employed by qualified experts. Judaism, for which the problem is similar, did not lack great halachists in the post-geonic period who challenged gaonic enactments as contrary to the Talmud. An outstanding example is Maimonides with his Code, the *Mishne Torah*. Today, especially in Israel, many responsible traditionalists appeal for a return to the Talmud in order to find a solution for the many halachic difficulties of life in a sovereign independent modern state.

I spoke of parallelism and not of influence since it is obvious that in the gaonic period the Muslim jurists could not have been aware of the development of the Jewish oral law from the *Tannaim* onwards, nor would their Jewish informants or advisers have suggested to them how to proceed. But all the same, the parallelism is not surprising; on the contrary, it is precisely what we would expect to happen in a system which is based on a revelation which had to serve as the ideal norm in a changing world and had to be respected as the fountainhead of a supplementary oral tradition which itself could only be developed by interpretation of Koran and *Sunna* with the help of rules of interpretation combined with independent judgment. The way from the *mujtahids* to the *muqallids* was as inevitable as that from the *Tannaim* to the *Amoraim* and *Saboraim*.

LEGAL FICTIONS

One of the means of keeping the Divine law in being and making a ruling in the interests of fairness and equity was the application of subterfuges (*ḥiyal*), which lead inevitably to casuistry. We find this in Judaism and in the Church with its canon law no less than in Islam. It is a corollary of applying justice in a climate of change not foreseen by the original lawgiver and the direct result of the inability to reconcile the law fixed at an earlier stage of moral and legal development with the imperative need, on ethical, social and economic grounds, to legislate contrariwise. It must needs appear to the strict believer that legal fiction, in the strict sense of the term, is still preferable to abandoning the axiom of the ideally perfect and absolutely binding revealed law of old.

CLASSES OF ACTIONS

One final point of contact between Muslim and Jewish law shall round off this first part of our survey of the fruitful encounter between a fully matured Judaism and a growing Islam.

Although the formulation is in strictly legal language and form, the actions which by commission or omission draw upon themselves certain legal consequences thus formulated are seen in an extra-legal context. Since the law is religious law and since religion finds its expression in ethics, all actions falling under the law are of necessity related to moral values, to Good or Evil. Hence they fall into five categories which are common to Judaism and Islam. They are the obligatory or compulsory, which corresponds in Judaism to *chova*; the commended—*mitsvat 'ase*; the permissible or indifferent—*r'shut*; the disapproved—*mitsvat lo ta 'aseh*; and the forbidden or prohibited—*issur*. This means that *Fiqh* and *Halacha* are each a *corpus* of religious duties, of commandments and prohibitions, and not law like Roman law.

THE HERITAGE

Enough has been said to show that there is, indeed, considerable common ground between Judaism and Islam,

much direct influence of Jewish concepts in religious doctrine and folklore and in religious law in principles, method
and legislation. Yet it cannot be too often repeated that in
addition there is much that is specifically Islamic going back
to Arab ideals and ideas which has produced a new faith.
Islam established itself alongside the older monotheistic religions sharing much with them, particularly with Judaism,
but differing from them sufficiently to develop into a powerful and independent religious force and into an imposing
religious culture and civilisation. In conquering older civilisations, it incorporated much of the material and spiritual
achievements of those it vanquished and thus preserved and
disseminated religious and moral values which would otherwise have remained confined to a smaller part of mankind
or would have perished altogether.

Islam has not only entered into the inheritance of Hebraic
culture in religion and ethics but has also become heir to
the culture and civilisation of Hellas. While its religious
sciences have been developed upon the basis of Hebraic
religion and ethics, the natural sciences and philosophy which
it developed stem from Greece and the Hellenistic world.
Islam has striven hard to bring the double inheritance to
a harmonious unity and has succeeded, as far as it was
possible to assimilate two systems which are in the last resort
irreconcilable since they start from opposite poles and are
rooted in different attitudes and values. But Islam was successful enough to become the teacher of the West largely
through Jewish intermediaries. It has absorbed Greek science
and philosophy as far as its indigenous *ethos* would allow and
has handed on both, though modified by its own basic outlook, again mainly through the creative transmission by
Jews whose basic outlook was so similar to that of their
Muslim masters.

The religious and the 'secular' sciences of medieval Islam

have stimulated Jews within its boundaries to prodigious feats of intellectual endeavour which resulted in the first systematic presentation of Jewish religious and ethical values. Jews cultivated their own religious sciences which they firmly established, or developed and consolidated in the case of law, and handed them on to future generations of Jews including our own. Although their form is timebound, their substance is of permanent value. Medieval Jews under Islam also made an important contribution to the natural sciences and to philosophy as independent disciples of the Muslim disciples of the Greek and Hellenistic masters. They transmitted to the West this Greek-Hellenistic legacy in a form sufficiently recognisable to prepare the ground for the Renaissance and to lead Western thinkers and scholars to the clear springs of Greek and Hellenistic thought. Muslims and Jews advanced medicine, science and philosophy appreciably and lastingly.

Though the last point cannot here be developed, it must, however, at least be stated. In the field of the religious sciences (biblical exegesis, *Halachah*, philosophy and theology and religious poetry (and even secular poetry as well)) Islam has, to repeat, stimulated and guided Jewish thinkers and teachers. This shall form the subject of the second part of our survey.

Part Two

★

JUDAISM UNDER ISLAM

JUDAISM UNDER ISLAM

*

JEWISH LAW

It is a fact that the strict adherence to traditional Judaism has contributed more than any other factor to the survival of Judaism and the Jews. It is, therefore, obvious that contact with other cultures and civilisations is bound to leave its mark in the *corpus* of halachic literature. The reader who is familiar with Mishna and Talmud has only to remember not only a number of Greek and Latin loanwords, but even a few institutions such as Hillel's *Prosbul* and the *Afikoman* of the *Seder* to be aware of such living contact. The many *Loazim* or French loanwords in Rashi's classical commentary on the Talmud (and in his Bible commentary) testify equally vividly to the Jewish indebtedness to its environment even at a time so unpropitious and dangerous as the Crusades.

We will, therefore, not be surprised to find in the halachic activity of Jewry under Islam here and there an echo of its Muslim environment. It is for this practical reason—because of the paramount importance of the *Halachah*—that we begin our brief survey of the impact of the Islamic *milieu* on Judaism with Jewish law and not with Bible or philosophy and theology or poetry.

When speaking of the *fatwa* at the end of the first part, I hinted at the geonim and their halachic activity and contribution to the development of Jewish law and through it to the survival of Judaism.

It is well known that the gaonate as an institution and as

a part of communal organisation owes nothing to Islam. Even chronologically, the gaonic period precedes the conquest of Iraq (Babylonia) by Islam: we reckon the gaonic period from 589, and Iraq was won for Islam in 637. But until the end of this period of Jewish history in 1040 the geonim lived and worked in Sura and Pumbadita in an Islamic environment which has not only influenced the form of their decisions, but to some extent actually called certain of them into being. This has affected Jewry at large, since the writ of the gaonate ran throughout the world where Jewish communities lived and wanted to live in conformity with talmudic Judaism. From all over the world Jews flocked to the Babylonian seats of learning to listen to the discussions and interpretations of the Talmud at the two academies presided over by the geonim.

The geonim claimed to be the lawful successors of the presidents of the Sanhedrin in Jerusalem and on the strength of this authority demanded and received unquestioning obedience of their enactments and decisions. They based their decisions whenever possible on the Talmud, by whose authoritative exposition they secured the unbroken continuity of Jewish life. But at times new circumstances demanded new solutions which, being without precedent, could not be found without departing from the Talmud. The geonim admitted such departure from tradition and justified it with the principle of "the adjustment of human relations", another talmudic principle of the type discussed earlier on, which was devised to enable Judaism to remain true to its basic principles while on the plane of inter-human relations compromise could be tolerated and was in fact essential. Things only start to go wrong when the principles are being forgotten and adjustments are being made without reference to fundamentals of belief, conviction and ethical conduct. This applies to all periods of Jewish history, including our own age. The talmudic principles come pretty close to the Islamic principle of *inṣāf*, discussed in the first part. They have to be taken in conjunction with the further ruling, already quoted, that "the law of government is law". This principle applied in the main to litigation involving Jews with non-Jews and the geonim made strenuous efforts to keep inter-Jewish strife and dispute within the jurisdiction of the Jewish courts and urged Jewish litigants to bring their disputes before their own courts. Apart from everything else, this was imperative in order to ensure and maintain religious, social and cultural autonomy.

That the authority of the geonim should be recognised throughout the realm of the caliphate goes without saying. For Jewish autonomy was recognised and the Exilarch was accorded royal honours at the court of the Caliph in Bagdad. He was "the head of the Captivity" (*resh galuta*), claimed Davidic descent and thus personified the continuity of Jewish national existence. For the Jews he personified their Messianic hope of final restoration to *Erets Yisrael*; to the Caliph he was responsible for the full and prompt payment of the fiscal obligations of the Jews as *dhimmis*. Spiritual authority rested with the two geonim, and although the powers of Exilarch and geonim did not overlap and the Exilarch had no control over religious matters, a clash of personalities was at times inevitable. This was due in part to the fact that the Caliph insisted that the geonim confirm the election of the Exilarch by the Jewish people, but had to pay homage to the Exilarch at his solemn installation. While the independence of the Exilarch was thus severely curtailed under the caliphate and real authority rested with the geonim, a strong exilarchal personality might easily clash with a strong Gaon. Although the existence of two geonim goes back to the two outstanding talmudic sages Rav and Shemuel, the academy of Sura soon gained the ascendancy over that of Pumbadita. The president of Sura was recognised as the only holder of the presidential office until the death of R. Sa'adya Gaon who was known as *ha-Gaon*, the Gaon *par excellence*. The Gaon of Sura seems to have enjoyed freedom from exilarchal interference and financial independence. He acted as the Exilarch's deputy in case of a vacancy until a new Exilarch was elected.

The most serious conflict between an Exilarch and a Gaon of Sura was that between David ben Zakkai and Sa'adya. Although warned against Sa'adya's fearless independence of mind, the Exilarch appointed him in 928 to the vacant presidency of Sura, since he wanted to see the greatest living scholar guide the principal seat of learning. Two years later, the two men were already locked in a serious struggle which lasted for four years and involved Sa'adya's excommunication and deposition by the Exilarch. It ended with their reconciliation and was followed by another four years of peaceful co-operation until David ben Zakkai's death. The quarrel arose over litigation which the Exilarch had decided wrongfully to Sa'adya's mind. Consequently, Sa'adya refused to legalise this decision by his signature.

This incident shows that ultimate authority rested with the Gaon in legal matters. How were decisions arrived at and what form did they take?

THE GEONIC *RESPONSA*

It is clear from the foregoing that the geonim as presidents of the academies were the only scholars of recognised authority based on sound learning and expert knowledge of the Talmud, who could, through interpretation of the Talmud, decide fresh cases which arose in the new circumstances. Although the decision was theirs, it was in many cases arrived at after a democratic process of prolonged public discussion. Twice yearly at gatherings called *Kalla*, the scholars formed themselves into a "Great Sanhedrin" of seventy, presided over by the Gaon, and debated cases. Behind the president and the seventy there sat the other scholars of the academy and behind them often up to four hundred students. Many of the students came from abroad, not only from other provinces and countries of the vast Islamic empire of the Caliphs, but from even further afield, from western and central Europe. They listened to the interpretation of the Talmud and its application to matters of family law, or to ethical, social and commercial problems and took the decisions back to their country of origin to serve there as the norm or at least as the basis for decisions of local problems. For, as stated above, the authority of the Geonim of Babylonia was recognised by the scholars of the Jewish communities everywhere.

I am not aware that the *Muftis* arrived at their decisions in a similar manner; but this question awaits elucidation by a long overdue investigation. In any case, the form the decision of the geonim took resembles the *fatwa* so closely that we must assume Muslim influence. The *Responsa* (*teshuvot*) take the form of answers to questions (*she'elot*) put to the geonim. They possessed legal force which was binding throughout the geonic period, at any rate wherever Jewish law was observed. Only towards the close of the period when the authority of the geonim was on the wane owing to political unrest and upheavals threatening the caliphate and hastening its decline and fall, a critical attitude arises and stiffens; and the codifiers of Jewish law began to subject the gaonic decisions to a penetrating scrutiny in the light of the Talmud. If the decisions were found to be contrary to the Talmud, they were overruled.

The authority of the decision was helped not a little by

the language in which it was couched: the geonim certainly did not lack the assurance of Divine help, and in invoking God's help for their decision "according to the *Torah*" in the closing formula of an "answer" they had no doubt that their decision was in accordance with the *Torah* and was, therefore, valid and binding.

They exercised their great responsibility with integrity, resourcefulness, care and consideration. For they knew that the maintenance of a distinctly Jewish life and the survival of Judaism as a way of life depended on their ability to preserve the spirit of the *Torah* as enshrined in the Talmud, while paying humane attention to the needs of the time. To fit Judaism and Jewish communal and individual life into the system of *dhimma* under Islam required the courage and the ability to disregard the letter of the Law. Life in accordance with the Divine will as laid down in the *Torah* could only be lived if internal unity could be preserved on an appropriate level of high morality and intellectual endeavour. At the same time Jewish life had to be accommodated to external circumstances over which the spiritual leaders had no control. The only thing which could guide them was the recognition of *dhimma* and the expectation that if they kept their part of the contract they could count on the protection of the Muslim authorities. Internally, therefore, the geonim had to guard the purity of family life, honesty in commercial dealings, mutual social responsibility and help and co-operation and an adequate knowledge of Bible and Talmud to ensure a thriving intellectual life which could hold its own against the flowering of the spirit in Muslim society. This entailed the cultivation of theology and philosophy in living contact with Muslim intellectual life. The geonim had moreover to watch that a code of social and commercial morals was being scrupulously adhered to so that relations with Muslims in general and with the Islamic authorities in particular were good and proceeded with as little friction and tension as possible. For on these friendly relations the survival of Judaism and the smooth functioning of Jewish autonomy largely depended. This is clearly reflected in the *Responsa* of this period. To appreciate their significance it is necessary for us to glance quickly at Jewish life under Islam.

JEWISH PARTICIPATION IN THE LIFE OF MUSLIM SOCIETY

We have already heard that the Jews of Arabia were an integral part of Arab society before the rise of Islam. They were farmers, craftsmen and merchants. The rapid expansion of the Islamic empire by conquest and conversion presented the Arab rulers with many new problems of government and administration which could only be solved by the employment of Jews and Christians on a large scale until sufficient numbers of Muslims were trained to man the offices of state throughout the caliphate. Islam, as heir to Byzantium and Persia continued their forms of administration and many former officials stayed on as converts or as *dhimmis*. Iraq was, as stated earlier, the centre of Jewry and possessed a highly developed Jewish community. Artisans, bankers and merchants fulfilled necessary economic functions rousing the anger of theologians if they were employed by the Caliphs and their high dignitaries, and the envy of competitors. Jewish physicians were in great demand and no opposition on religious grounds could dislodge them from their positions of trust and usefulness. Conversionist zeal was strong; to resist the lure of social equality and material reward demanded strong conviction and a deep sense of loyalty to Judaism and to the community. The spiritual leaders of Muslim Jewry proved equal to the task. But the business of adjustment was protracted and delicate, for the Jews were integrated into Muslim society as nearly as was possible for *dhimmis*. It was naturally easier for physicians to be respected and accepted than it was for tax-farmers and tax-collectors, and it speaks well for the Muslims and their tolerance that by and large so relatively few outbursts of violence occurred. With the exception of two outbreaks in Spain, one in Cordova in 1013 and, a more serious one, in Granada in 1066, both of which were originally not directed against the Jews though they became the principal sufferers, there was only one concerted persecution. This was officially inspired by the fanatical Almohades who, in 1148, massacred whole Jewish communities in southern Spain. In Egypt, the Jews and the Christian Copts were, on occasion, subjected to mob violence, but only after Fatimid rule had declined and given way to insecurity and lawlessness. Thus, such outbursts occurred only in times of political unrest and instability. The end of the caliphate in 1258 in Bagdad spelt disaster and ruin, but not only for the Jews, as is evidenced by the Mongol invasions of the thirteenth and fourteenth centuries.

Long centuries of quiet enabled an economically sound, socially well organised and intellectually thriving community to make a signal contribution to law and lore, first in Babylonia, then in Spain, North Africa and Egypt.

Nor must we forget the considerable share Jewish commercial enterprise had in the economy of medieval Islam as we now know from many documents from the Cairo *Geniza*, made available and evaluated by S. D. Goitein. Jewish merchants braved the hazards of long sea voyages to India from other parts of the Muslim empire, such as Spain, North Africa, Egypt, Iraq and Persia and carried on a flourishing trade with both East and West. They could do this the more easily since one law bound the Jews of different countries together and partnership was built on more than economic interest.

Last but not least there is the Jewish share in the spreading of Greek and Hellenistic culture to the Christian West. All these activities would be unthinkable without the solid base of traditional Judaism fully attuned to the needs of the times. In the security of the all-embracing *Torah*, the systematic exploration and exposition of the fundamentals of Jewish belief and practice could be carried out for the first time, stimulated and helped by Muslim scholasticism which was built on the encounter with Greek science and philosophy.

LEGISLATING FOR THE TIMES

Naturally, the tempo of Islamic advance and absorption within its territory of divergent social patterns and economic activities dictated the pace of Jewish adjustment to the new masters and their way of life. To repeat, the aim was to preserve the Jewish way of life by retaining and clarifying the structure of belief and conviction so that Judaism should command the allegiance of its adherents. At the same time the challenge of the victorious faith and of the great opportunities it offered had to be met and utilised whenever and wherever possible for the strengthening of the inherited traditions so that the disadvantages of a tolerated minority would be outweighed by its vitality in keeping with the tendencies of the age. The task which faced the geonim was to make "the fence round the *Torah*" strong and Judaism within it impregnable while at the same time enabling the Jews to assimilate to their inherited culture that which was not only best in the world around them but would blend with their own attitude and ideas. They applied themselves to it with determination and to this end they added to the *Halachah*, enactments concerning those branches of civil law which Jewish autonomy was allowed to retain, and also concerning the *mores* of their community.

One of the important concerns for the guardians of Judaism was to insulate the community as much as possible from the Muslims, to keep the Jews within the fold by meeting their needs in such a way that they did not want to apply to a Muslim court. Thus, the geonim permitted a letter of divorce to be issued to an unmanageable wife at once instead of after a waiting period of twelve months in accordance with a talmudic ruling. If they had not done so, Jewish wives desirous of obtaining a divorce would have applied to a Muslim court.

In the realm of commercial law they introduced an oath to be sworn by a debtor that he could not pay his creditor. The rapid growth of trade and commerce and the opportunities thus afforded for quick and large profits favoured a trend to exchange landed property for movables. To meet the new situation, the geonim had to take appropriate measures for the preservation of agricultural estates in Jewish hands. On the other hand, they had to protect not only the debtors, as we have just seen, but also the creditors. This was especially necessary in view of the risks and hazards involved in overseas trade. Legislation had to fix the liability in case of death and had to protect the heirs of the deceased. This was achieved by the introduction of special oaths, and by a number of penalties, among them the ban (*Cherem*). We are told of a case where the Gaon had to decide whether a ban pronounced by a local Jewish court by order of the Muslim ruler was valid or not. The ban prohibited the property, which the ruler wished to confiscate, being handed over to the rightful heirs of the deceased. The criterion by which the Gaon could decide this difficult question was obviously the principle of *dina demalchuta dina*. He ruled that in this case *the law of the government* was not *law* since the king had no legal right to his action: the ban had been pronounced under threat of illegal force and was, therefore, invalid.

The economic activity of Jews under Islam is interestingly described and analysed by S. D. Goitein in Chapter 6 of his book *Jews and Arabs*: "The economic transformation and communal reorganisation of the Jewish people in Islamic times".

Examples could be multiplied, but enough has been said to stress the great importance of a flexible Jewish law in a rapidly changing world.

Contact with Islam worked, as we know, in both directions, and local custom was a factor to reckon with even in the strongly guarded sphere of religious ceremonies. If they could not succeed in eliminating them because they were too deeply rooted in popular imagination the rabbis always tried to make such customs innocuous. Their guiding principle was to integrate popular customs which were not easily reconcilable with Jewish concepts in Judaism by giving them a deeper spiritual meaning in accord with Jewish ethics.

CODIFICATION OF LAW

The *Responsa* grew into a considerable body of new legislation which varied from country to country as it had to take into account local customs. This fact, together with the example of monographs and handbooks of groups and branches of law originating in the four Muslim schools of law, favoured a tendency among halachists to bring the multitude of enactments into a systematically ordered book. This was to help the expert to find a ready solution to legal questions and to have a reliable guide to the law as it stood in his day, compared with the Talmud. In this way a whole literature of codes came into being. It greatly helped to preserve unity in diversity all over the Jewish world and served not only as a much needed basis for legal practice but also for continuous development and thus guaranteed the flexibility and adequacy of Jewish law at all times. *Fiqh*, which owes so much to Judaism, in turn helped Jewish specialists from the ninth century onwards to systematise the *Halachah*. The work of making collections of *halachot* had already begun in the eighth century and culminated in the collection *Halachot Gedolot* after several generations of geonim had been engaged in this practical task. It goes without saying that the already mentioned Sa'adya Gaon (882-942) left many *Responsa* dealing with ritual and economic matters and also a treatise on the laws governinig inheritance. This is the first book devoted to a legal topic of great importance in an age of economic change. In arrangement it shows clearly the impact of *Fiqh*. He also dealt systematically and comprehensively with such topics as obligations and usury in similar treatises.

MAIMONIDES'S CODE OF JEWISH LAW

This formal influence is especially discernible in the great Code of the greatest medieval Jewish thinker and Halachist, the *Mishne Torah* or *Yad haChazaka* of Maimonides (1135-1204) which must be briefly outlined at least. Its arrangement in fourteen books not only shows the pattern of *Fiqh*-classification, but Maimonides's development of the application of the 'roots' of *Fiqh*, in particular of *ijmā'* with *isnād*, *consensus* and chain of tradition, both of which, as we have seen earlier on, have come from Judaism into Islam.

Maimonides re-introduced them in the greatly expanded form of the *Ḥadīth*. Thus he managed to produce an unbroken chain of tradition from Moses to Rav Ashi to whom we owe the sifting and assembly of the material of the Talmud. Owing to the nature of Jewish law which is determined by its divine origin, and to its range over the whole life of man in relation to God and to his fellow men, we cannot expect a Jewish law code to look like a code of Roman law. Maimonides's Code was preceded by his "Book of Commandments", the first scientific exposition of the six hundred and thirteen *Mitsvot*. His Code comes at the end of centuries' old development without which it would not have been possible. But it would be unthinkable also without Maimonides's systematic, lucid mind. His Code, though fiercely attacked for simply stating the law without recording the discussion which led to it, has served as the model for all subsequent codification of Jewish law, including the *Shulchan Aruch* of Joseph Karo, which is still valid today.

In form, Maimonides's Code displays the synthesis of Greek philosophy in its Aristotelian perfection of systematic clear thinking and method, with the traditional interpretation of the written *Torah* and its peculiar method of legal argumentation. Maimonides reduced the unwieldy bulk of *Halachah* to a succinct, well ordered whole in pure mishnaic Hebrew.

The exposition of valid *Halachah* in its entirety is preceded by a philosophical discussion of the fundamental beliefs and convictions of Judaism which has a striking resemblance with his *Guide for the Perplexed*. He is concerned with the end of man, who has received the commandments in order to achieve the knowledge and love of God as much as is in man's power. The knowledge of Reality fills the faithful with admiration for God's wisdom and with awe for His

E

might and power; it leads him to serve God in love. It ensures his ultimate happiness of which the philosophers speak but which only the divinely revealed perfect *Torah* of Moses can guarantee through the fulfilment of its commandments. It is not possible to discuss here the principles Maimonides has laid down for testing valid *Halachah*. Suffice it to mention in what his signal contribution to the clarification of Jewish law and to its further development as a code of ethics and a discipline for the good life consists. He starts from the Talmud as the natural basis and immovable centre of a God-centred Jewish life. But he claims for himself and his generation what every generation—unfortunately excepting the past few generations including our own—of conscious, traditional Jews has considered its rightful duty: to reinterpret the Talmud for the needs of his time and in the language appropriate to it. Each generation made laws and regulations to meet the requirements of the moment in matters of forbidden and permitted, binding and voluntary. He also made full allowance for custom.

Since, according to the Rabbis, "the *Torah* speaks in the language of men", the original *mitsvot* are necessarily in need of fresh interpretation in accord with the changing conditions of life. They were aforetimes proclaimed in a language which our forefathers could understand: they were meant to help them on their way to know and to love God in the particular conditions prevailing in their day. But if their text is timebound, their meaning and validity is permanent and eternally binding upon all those who live under the *Torah*. They can retain their authority only if they are made clear to subsequent generations of Jews in the context of their time and circumstances.

The rules of interpretation evolved by the teachers of the Mishna must be applied again and again to elicit the meaning of the commandments and to show how they must be observed to fulfil their function. This function has remained unchanged through the ages: it is to help man attain his end, the highest good.

In the age of Maimonides, the intellectual climate was determined by the philosophy of Plato and Aristotle and their commentators and successors, as understood and explained by the Muslim religious philosophers. Maimonides considered it his right and his plain duty to enlist this knowledge of the universe in the service of explaining the *Torah* to his generation. He pressed the knowledge of physics, mathematics, astronomy, agriculture, of politics and ethics and metaphysics, into the service of expounding the *Torah* as the perfect guide to God and to man's perfection in His service. The Rabbis of Mishna and Talmud could never have fixed the *Halachah* without the knowledge of the natural sciences of their age. Their knowledge was timebound and often inadequate, even wrong judged by the knowledge available to him. He, therefore, claimed the right to give a better explanation with the help of that knowledge at his disposal.

The idea, to write an introduction to all the orders of the Talmud in which he set out methodically the principles which underlie the regulations and brought out their significance within the system, was not new. Shemuel haNagid, chief minister of the Muslim ruler of Granada in the middle of the eleventh century, had written an introduction to the Talmud. There are the *Halachot* of Isaac Alfasi (from Fez in North Africa) who, in his old age, transplanted the systematic study of the Talmud to Spain. But more nearly akin in spirit to Maimonides's work is the "Introduction to the Talmud" of Shemuel ben Chofni at the very end of the gaonate in Babylonia who wrote his halachic works in Arabic and shows the influence of *Fiqh* in his concentration on and elucidation of the principles of the *Halachah*.

While coming after these scholars, Maimonides surpassed them all in his masterly grasp of the essentials of the law in all its ramifications. Besides, he used his method in order to make clear the purpose of all commandments, namely, to lead man to his perfection by serving God in action and in thought. His philosophical bent made him attach great importance to the theoretical commandments of the *Torah*. He was anxious that sound beliefs and right convictions should be man's foremost concern and that through them he should draw near to the divine creator and ruler of the Universe. But his theoretical preoccupation did not lead him to neglect the practical side of the commandments: the essential unity of theory and practice was for him never in doubt. In fact, he insists that just as the *chacham*, the wise and learned man, is distinguished from others by his knowledge and understanding, so must he excel in the joyous fulfilment of the practical commandments of personal and social life. He must be an example to others. When discussing religious philosophy we shall have to say a good deal more about this ideal of the unity of thought and action.

By identifying the *Torah* with wisdom in the wake of the Hebrew wisdom literature and of the age of Hellenism, especially of Philo of Alexandria, the medieval Jewish thinkers legitimised the study of Greek and Hellenistic philosophy in its Arabic garb and considered it their rightful duty to explain the *Torah* with its help. If *Torah* is wisdom there can be no conflict between them: both teach the same truth which is one and indivisible, only in different ways.

What is important is the use made by Maimonides of the categories of philosophical thought, of its method and of its findings, for the elucidation of Bible and Talmud. Hence he prefaces his codification of Jewish law by a theoretical disquisition on the fundamental beliefs and convictions of

Judaism in the *Sefer haMadda'*. For tradition and philosophy are agreed that without belief in the oneness and unity of God, the creator out of nothing, the God of love and mercy, of justice and righteousness, the performance of the Commandments would have neither justification nor meaning. God rewards and punishes His servant in accordance with his voluntary obedience or disobedience to the Divine will expressed in the *Torah*; but He has sent His prophets to show the way to the sinner: through repentance he may gain forgiveness. No less essential a belief is the Jew's faith in ultimate redemption through the promised Messiah of the house of David. Man must know these basic teachings and accept them; only then has his fulfilment of the practical commandments meaning and purpose. Maimonides's philosophical superstructure explains the true significance of the *Torah* to which the lucid presentation of the minute details of the commandments is related. It is the function of the *Halachah* to teach man the application of these great principles of Judaism and their realisation in a God-centred life.

Abraham, the beloved of God, is for Maimonides— possibly with a polemical intention against Islam—the personification of man's ideal expressed in the *Torah* by the commandment "And thou shalt love the Lord thy God ..." It is love of God which inspires man to study and fulfil the commandments. Love of God manifests itself in study to discover the truth not to gain prestige and riches; in practising "the joy of the commandment" not from fear of evil or hope of reward, but to serve God. Maimonides stresses the intellectual basis of love: knowledge. But he knows that men are different and that, therefore, their knowledge is unequal. But religion offers to every believer a unique aid to knowledge: prophetic revelation and divine providence. Thus it not only draws a clear distinction between God's knowledge and man's knowledge, which share nothing but

a name; it also aids the intellectually less strong in his desire
to know and love and fear God by showing him the way
through God's miraculous providence and exalted wisdom
which are taught in the *Torah* for everybody to see and to
comprehend. Ultimately, the nature of God is unfathom-
able, but religious experience can bring man a deeper
insight.

Maimonides admits the rabbinic distinction of the commandments into duties towards God and duties to one's
fellow men, but he subordinates the latter to the former.
Every commandment aims at ethical improvement, at right
conduct, at knowledge and understanding and thus man, by
keeping it, fulfils his duty to God at the same time. Knowledge leads to good deeds, good deeds increase knowledge
and increased knowledge leads to love of God.

He was not satisfied with relating every commandment to
the higher purpose of conscious service in knowledge and
love. He also wanted to know the reason for every commandment if that were possible. His rational bent came into
conflict in this particular with the ancient Rabbis and their
followers among his own contemporaries who deprecated
this probing into the underlying reasons for commandments. That they were given by God was sufficient reason
to observe them. Though admitting the limitations of the
human intellect, Maimonides sought a rational justification
for the commandments. Since the *Torah* could not contain
anything which ran counter to reason, he was forced, like
Saʿadya and others before him, to look for a hidden, inner
meaning of Scripture when the literal meaning did not
satisfy his reasoning. No wonder that his rational explanation
of the sacrifices shocked some of his contemporaries as contrary to tradition. Yet, it would be wrong to imagine that
Maimonides questioned the validity of any commandment:
for him, as for all adherents to traditional Judaism, the *Torah*

as a whole was divinely revealed and obligatory on all in every detail.

His contemporaries objected not only to the prominence which Maimonides seemed to give to human reason, but for quite another reason as well. He had the audacity simply to lay down the law without giving the reasons for his decisions and without citing authorities—possibly under the impact of his Muslim surroundings. This was a revolutionary innovation which was bound to rouse justifiable opposition. For the continuous development of the *Halachah*, its flexibility and adaptability to the needs of the time largely depended on discussion and on the knowledge of previous discussion which led to a legal decision. Maimonides had no intention to set the Talmud aside, to stifle discussion and to rule out development and change. But he was faced with a great mass of decisions of individual problems and questions and he felt the imperative need to bring order into what could lead to confusion if remaining unchecked. He wanted to lay down the law for practical purposes, to provide a reliable guide for the judge. But he was not infallible, and just as he criticised geonic decisions as contrary to the Talmud, despite his reverence and respect for them, his own decisions might be questioned by contemporary and later legal experts who were charged with the interpretation of the *Halachah*.

It is an open question whether it would not have been better if his Code had not led to the *Shulchan Aruch's* authority, with all that it entails for the legislative process. "Custom precedes law" and "custom annuls law" can only have meaning or re-acquire meaning if the law is not fixed and static.

But, in his time, Maimonides's Code was a great boon; it did much to cement and maintain the unity of Jewry under Islam and beyond, and it has helped to consolidate the rule of one law from the Mediterranean to the Indian Ocean. His reverent but critical attitude to the geonim has done much to re-open the discussion of the Talmud whose authority Maimonides upheld against them if necessary, as, for instance, in the question of the Liturgy. By his own codification, he has shown the way not only to subsequent codifiers but to all later generations by establishing the principle and practice of going back to the Talmud over later timebound decisions.

It is for the halachists of our time to decide how Jewish law today can be rejoined to the Talmud. As long as we remember that the Talmud represents a stage in the development of Jewish law and not the final achievement we may be able to frame a workable law for our time, on the basis of talmudic principles if not on that of actual legislation. This I think Maimonides taught us. He was helped by the methods of *Fiqh* and its codification, but he was motivated by the desire to provide his generation with the lucid presentation of valid law which should guide them as Jews within Muslim culture and civilisation both in thought and action. He was aware that what was to be believed had to be clear, just as the rules of conduct had to be precise and unequivocal. He was also aware that, even under Islam, law could not stand still and that geonic legislation required modification in certain detail. This he strove to obtain by the strict application of talmudic principles. His attitude to and treatment of geonic legislation shows that nothing in the realm of law can ever be final since the conditions which called it forth are not stationary. The more reason so it seems to set out the fundamentals of Judaism which must always remain the same. The conviction that as long as they were clear and accepted the moral basis of conduct was secure and changes in practice were possible, even necessary, is surely sound and capable of serving as a pattern at all times. Here even more than in the strictly practical-legal matter of his Code lies its permanent significance. It is true that the geonim also strove to remain as close to the talmudic legislation as possible. As we saw a little earlier, one of the last of them, Shemuel ben Chofni was already concerned with the principles of the Talmud. Once his work is made available by the labours of Prof. D. H. Baneth, we shall be able to see how close he was to Maimonides.

In conclusion, it can be said that Maimonides's Code shows the impact of Islam in its form, but the substance is Jewish. It seems to me that this is also the result of life under Islam. The need to state the theoretical basis of Judaism is due not only to the desire to place practical law within a framework of belief and conviction which gives it purpose and significance. It is also due to the significant place theology and philosophy occupied in Muslim society at that moment. That Maimonides evolved his thirteen principles of faith is another example of the preoccupation with the principles of faith and not only with its practice. Moreover, it is in conformity with contemporary tendencies in Islam. For this reason, we need only consider his Code together with his philosophical main work, the *Guide for the Perplexed*, to realize that under Islam in the twelfth century Judaism could not have survived by the mere observance of the *mitsvot* unaided by the awareness of their meaning. Their observance testified to the vitality of the "despised religion" —to borrow a term from the title of Yehuda Halevi's *Kuzari* written a century earlier. Judaism had already to fight for its life in the ninth, tenth and eleventh centuries. The challenge of Islam had to be met; it was the more incisive because it contained so much that was Jewish. Yet, apologetics and polemics apart—and they played their part— the positive statement of Judaism as a way of life had a profound effect on its subsequent development as well. The challenge of Islam has thrown up not only halachists, but also philologists, commentators, poets and philosophers.

HEBREW AND BIBLE STUDY

Baghdad was famed in the ninth century for a great flowering of the spirit. Acquaintance with Greek philosophy through translations had caused a ferment among the Muslims, and not only did the presence of three monotheistic religions produce propaganda and controversy, but the encounter with philosophy produced a critical attitude to one's own faith no less than to that of others. The tolerance of early Islam naturally had its two sides, as toleration always has. It cannot flourish in an atmosphere where one faith claims a monopoly of truth. But if we grant the other faiths also some truth, even if we think ours possesses the same truth in greater perfection, we open the door to scepticism and to doubt. This happened in the Baghdad of Al-Ma'mun, the Abbasid Caliph. Representatives of the three faiths, Islam, Judaism and Christianity, met to discuss the merits of each on a strictly rational basis. Reason, not revealed dogma, was to be the final arbiter as well as the method of argument.

It would lead us too far to follow in detail the whole extent of the invasion of rational argument into every branch of the religious sciences. The rational approach deeply affected the science of exegesis of the Koran and, thus, also biblical exegesis. Reason played an increasing part in the controversy between Muslims and Jews about the veracity of the koranic version of biblical stories. Alongside with it there went a rationalist Muslim attack on the Koran, which found an echo in Judaism, in the attack of Chivi of Balch against the Bible. He raised two hundred objections to the biblical text, wanted to explain the miracles rationally as natural events and took exception to the description of God in the Bible. He naturally roused the opposition of the traditionalists, Rabbanites as well as Karaites. A fierce struggle raged round the Bible: Rabbinic Judaism had to fight not only against Muslim controversialists, but also against Jewish heretics, rationalists like Chivi, and the afore-mentioned Karaites who denied the validity of the Oral *Torah* and insisted on the exclusive authority of the written *Torah*. (That they had to develop their own *Halachah* does not concern us here.)

One of the principal opponents of the Karaites was Sa'adya Gaon who had also written a treatise against Chivi of Balch. The Karaites forced the Rabbanite majority to pay close attention to the literal meaning of the Bible. They themselves made important contributions to biblical exegesis, not least by grammatical and lexicographical studies. Without the existence of a well-developed science of the Arabic language which largely arose in connection with the exegesis of the Koran, Hebrew linguistics could hardly have been cultivated. In terminology and arrangement, in treatment of problems and in the solution of difficulties the Jews were dependent on the Arab grammarians. From the beginning, the study of the Hebrew language was closely linked with the interpretation of the Hebrew Bible and it has remained so to this day.

HEBREW PHILOLOGY

Sa'adya's pioneering efforts in grammar and lexicography laid the foundations for his own commentaries and for the whole medieval exegesis, in Spain, in Provence and in Northern France and Germany. Without the better understanding of the structure of Hebrew, the application of the method of *peshat* could not have reached its importance not only as a help towards the accurate understanding of Scripture, but also as a sharp weapon in the defence of Judaism which is based on the Bible against Christian and Muslim attack and attempts at conversion.

Not much of Sa'adya's philological output is extant. But when the centre of Jewish culture shifted from Babylonia to Spain, Hebrew grammar and lexicography were developed to a high degree, based on Sa'adya's work and, as already stated, on Arabic treatises. A lasting, scientifically sound foundation was laid for the systematic study of Hebrew and through it of the Bible. The demarcation line between *peshat* and *derash*, between the literal and the figurative, inner meaning of Scripture, became sharper and *peshat* in the strict meaning of the word begins in the wake of Sa'adya, continues with Rashi and attains its apogee with Abraham ibn Ezra and David Kimchi. The intensive study of Hebrew in the West begins with Menachem ben Saruk (about 960) and his very distinguished and able critic Dunash ibn Labrat, the disciple of Sa'adya. Dunash came to Cordova at the age of thirty and enjoyed the patronage of Chasdai ibn Shaprut. Dunash attacked Menachem's Hebrew dictionary, *machberet* which, a hundred years later, served *the* commentator of the Bible, Rashi, as a principal source and basis for his own linguistic studies. We learn from Menachem's introduction to the *machberet* that in his attempt at presenting the meaning and formation of the Hebrew roots he was guided by reason and study. He consulted the context. He shares with Sa'adya the idea of the unity of the Hebrew language and likewise often explains a Biblical word by a Mishnaic one. Dunash bases his attack on Menachem on his own comprehensive, systematic examination of morphology, grammar and syntax, aided by a comparative study of Arabic, Aramaic (of the *Targum*) and Talmud), the Massora and the rules of interpretation of the Rabbis. The halachist Sa'adya had naturally preceded him in this, but lacked his disciple's comprehensiveness. Dunash works towards the theory of three root letters and he attempts to replace biliteral by triliteral roots. He and his opponent exerted a strong influence on their respective disciples. Chayyūj, pupil and adherent of Menachem, established an authority far greater than that of his master and Dunash. He succeeded in establishing the triliteral theory scientifically, applied it to the so-called 'weak' verbs and established laws and rules for the vowel changes and the different grammatical forms. He wrote an important treatise on the 'weak' verbs and tells us in the introduction that he confined himself to the text of the Bible and usually drew conclusions from textual evidence as to what he did not find in the text. He greatly advanced our knowledge of morphology and verbal structure and also our understanding of the noun through extensive massoretic studies. Unlike Menachem and Dunash in his attack on the *machberet*, he wrote in Arabic and employs the terminology of Arabic grammar.

His work was completed by Ibn Janāh, known in Hebrew as Rabbi Jonah. He set out to complete the work of his master Chayyūj, but through many original observations and further researches he was able to produce a major work in two parts, a grammar and a dictionary. The latter under the title *Book of Roots* was long forgotten owing to David Kimchi's treatise of the same title which became the model for Hebrew dictionaries of Europe's Christian Hebraists and was the principal source for their study of the Bible until modern times.

R. Jonah used his linguistic knowledge to evaluate rabbinic biblical exegesis and by his attention to the style and diction of the Bible he furthered its correct understanding. Joseph Kimchi, David's father, depended on R. Jonah.

Moses ibn Gikatilla was a disciple of Chayyūj, whose principal studies he may have translated into Hebrew. He brought his linguistic knowledge to bear on his exegetical work which is, however, known to us only through quotations transmitted in the works of Abraham ibn Ezra.

INTERPRETATION OF THE BIBLE

The Bible, as the source of the *Halachah* and as an integral part of the liturgy, if for no other reason, would always command first place in Judaism. In fact, its study is a commandment, as we know from the sixth chapter of Deuteronomy, which calls upon the father to teach his children all the commandments, statutes and ordinances of the *Torah*. Teaching comprises what the text says as well as what it means. Leo Baeck expressed the truism that much of Jewish literature is interpretation of the Bible thus: "It is a principle in Judaism that truth has to be discovered in, and through, the Bible. The book of 'revelation' must again and again be revealed by the teacher. For every sentence and story in this book not only tells something, it also means something. It does not merely describe what has been and has now ceased to be. It manifests something permanent that attains actuality again and again."

The first requirement of this unending process of keeping and renewing *Torah* as a "tree of life" is to know and understand its plain meaning. Here Sa'adya has rendered a service that can hardly be exaggerated. Not only his Arabic translation of and his commentaries on several of its books sustained Arabic-speaking Jews who lived under Islam. He greatly influenced all students of the Bible who came after him, in Spain and North Africa, who in turn carried his message into France.

He combined several sources of knowledge into the first systematic exposition of the Bible's legal, ethical and theological teachings. We would expect the Gaon of Sura to be well versed in the traditional exposition of the Bible. We spoke of the linguistic approach he adopted to get at the plain sense of the text. Moreover, he made full use of the secular knowledge of his age, steeped as he was in the culture of his Muslim surroundings. Karaites, rationalists and Muslim controversialists combined to force upon the acknowledged leader of rabbinic Judaism the task of interpreting the Bible authoritatively, in conformity with Reason and Tradition. He starts from the unity of the whole Bible as the repository of the Divine revelation, as a guide to man in belief and action. Likewise, he insists on the unity of the individual books of the Bible. How he achieved this unity in his presentation cannot be demonstrated here nor can the many theological and philosophical digressions be illustrated. But a word must be said about his approach and method in general. According to him, knowledge has three roots: sense-perception, reason or rational perception, and necessary logical deduction. This secular knowledge of the philosopher is contrasted with the knowledge of the religious thinker and interpreter of Scripture who, as a member of the "community of the believers in the (absolute) unity (of God)" must needs add a fourth root: true, reliable tradition contained in the *Torah* and the Prophets. He insists on the complementary unity of Reason, *Torah* as the book of divine instruction, and Tradition. This tradition naturally contains the three 'secular' roots. But they cannot guarantee the character of absolute truth, since man's reason and experience are not perfect and reliable. Therefore tradition must possess an additional element, that of truth revealed to the prophets by God. Thus, Sa'adya says in the introduction to his Arabic version of the Pentateuch that God has given

man, in addition to the *Torah* and the Prophets, Reason
which precedes and Tradition which follows Revelation.
"With the help of the argument from reason, man realises
that God, who created everything out of nothing, is One,
Eternal and Unique, non-material, possessed of free will and
(absolutely) just." Tradition confirms this, and the traditional
laws are not in conflict with Reason. This is also the position
of medieval Jewish religious philosophy, likewise founded by
Sa'adya in his "Beliefs and Convictions" (*Emunot VeDe'ot*).
The antagonist of Reason is Nature, not Revelation, as he
states in his Arabic version of *Proverbs*: "When man's reason
rules over his nature he is truly human, if it is the other way
round, his actions are like that of beasts". To make reason
prevail over nature man must constantly strive for more and
more knowledge. Sa'adya was not only concerned with the
refutation of the rationalist *critique* of the very foundations
of the Bible, he was convinced that man as a rational
creature could only attain his purpose by using his intellect
rightly. Only through the intelligent, conscious fulfilment
of the commandments could man reach his goal : happiness.
Sa'adya developed this theme primarily in his philosophical-
theological *Emunot VeDe'ot*. But in his Arabic version and
interpretation of the Hebrew Bible he insists on the in-
adequacy of human reason for achieving man's happiness
unaided by revelation: study of the *Torah* is essential and
study requires instruction which is, for Sa'adya, of three
kinds. The first kind consists of command and prohibition;
the second informs the pupil, that is, the student of the
Torah, of the consequences of command and prohibition: by
man's free choice between obedience and disobedience he
receives reward or punishment. "This is stronger than the
first, for he can imagine the happiness or misfortune he will
reap in every deed he chooses." The third kind adds: "the
story of those people who obey the commandments, for

their reward and their happiness are the best, and the story of those people who injure themselves through their disobedience and are punished and unhappy. This way is stronger than the two former ways, for experience and test come to him who obeys ... and it takes for him the place of a testimony". The "seeker after wisdom"—Sa'adya's name for Proverbs—must, however, not inquire into the two problems which the Rabbis of old had already forbidden: creation and revelation, the Hebrew *ma'ase bereshit* and *ma'ase merkavah*. Instead, the wise advise the seeker: "Inquire into God's commandments and prohibitions and into what your fathers have handed down". This means that 'wisdom' is encompassed by *Torah* and Tradition.

Sa'adya was the first Rabbanite Bible commentator to bring a scientific linguistic analysis to bear on the content of the biblical books. With the help of grammar and lexicography and a close attention to the *Targum*, he set out to expound the Bible for the moral and intellectual instruction and edification of his generation. He concentrated on the literal meaning and permitted himself to depart from it only if a literal interpretation—as, for instance, of the bodily attributes of God, anthropomorphism—would be in conflict with reason and tradition. In this case, an inner meaning of a word or a passage had to be sought and found by recourse to rational argument.

This method and approach became the pattern for biblical exegesis in the Muslim East and West and exerted a lasting influence on that in the Christian West with Spain acting as the bridge to the non-Arabic-speaking Jews of France and Germany.

The effect of Sa'adya's biblical exegesis is strongly felt in the exegetical works of his Karaite opponents. But this cannot be described in detail.

Shemuel ben Chofni, whom we mentioned earlier, wrote

F

a philosophical commentary on the *Torah* and on some of the Prophets. Indeed a school of biblical exegesis arose in the the lifetime of Sa'adya in North Africa. Isaac Israeli, better known as a physician and philosopher, wrote an extensive commentary on the first chapter of Genesis. We know from his pupil Dunash ibn Tamim that his master was in correspondence with Sa'adya during the latter's stay in Egypt. Dunash ibn Tamim, like the grammarian Yehudah ibn Kuraish engaged in linguistic analysis of Biblical Hebrew. Both adopted and enlarged Sa'adya's comparative method by turning to Aramaic, later Hebrew and Arabic, in their explanation of biblical roots.

A link between Sa'adya and Bachya ben Asher, the disciple of Nachmanides, is provided, though indirectly, through the commentaries of Chananel ben Chushiel. Actually, we know of Chananel's work only through the quotations in Bachya ben Asher's commentary on the *Torah*.

Sa'adya's influence in the West will be discussed presently. Sa'adya's innovation of introducing his commentary on the various books of the Bible by a description of the contents and message and by setting out the difficulties of text and ideas expressed, was—despite Abraham ibn Ezra, Nachmanides and Gersonides—not fully taken up and perfected until Don Isaac Abravanel on the threshold of the Renaissance.

HISTORICAL EXEGESIS

In his insistence on the unity of the whole Bible and of its individual books Sa'adya found himself in complete agreement with Jewish tradition. Recourse to history to explain prophetic predictions, warnings and promises was not part of his technique. An appeal to history to cast doubt upon or

even reject the ascription of books or parts of books to individual authors would never have entered his mind. The
scepticism mentioned earlier engendered by the comparative
study of religion in Muslim intellectual society in which
Jews took an active share, sooner or later inevitably led to
a critical attitude towards the Bible on historical grounds.
Such an attitude was first adopted by Chivi of Balch, as we
saw. His tendency was clearly heretical and was aimed at
undermining not only the veracity of the Bible and its
ethical standards, but Judaism as a whole. But a critical
attitude need not endanger the revelational and authoritative
character of the Bible as the basis of Judaism at all. This is
evident from Abraham ibn Ezra, but can already be seen in
one of his important precursors in Spain, the aforementioned
Moses ibn Gikatilla. He appears to be the first Jewish commentator to assign the prophecies of the "Second Isaiah", i.e.
from chapter forty onwards, to the Babylonian Exile and
the time of the Second Temple. Altogether, he is inclined
to assign the prophecies of other prophets, such as Joel,
Obadia and Micah, to definite periods; according to him for
instance, Micah's messianic prophecies have the Second
Temple in mind. Of more far-reaching importance is his
rational explanation of the miracles in the Bible. He does not
deny their miraculous character but attempts a rational
explanation which takes account of the laws of nature.
Thus, the famous passage, Joshua 10.12 ff. in his view does
not mean that the sun and the moon actually stood still, but
that the reflection of the light of the sun lingered longer on
earth than usual and thus enabled the Children of Israel to
pursue the enemy and win the battle. This explanation
satisfies Moses ibn Gikatilla's religious belief that God inter-
vened at the behest of Joshua to aid Israel and grant him
victory, and at the same time enables our commentator to
hold fast to the scientific view that the sun and the moon are

in continuous movement. His contemporary Yehuda ibn
Balaam objected to this view. Both commentators influenced Abraham ibn Ezra, who had a high opinion of
Moses ibn Gikatilla whom he quotes—our only source for
ibn Gikatilla, whose writings are no longer extant.

RATIONAL EXEGESIS—*PESHAṬ*

Abraham ibn Ezra, who died in 1167, deserves mention
not only in his own right as one of our most important and
influential mediaeval Bible exegetes but also for his valuable
work of transmitting the epoch-making results of the
Spanish school of interpretation based on Hebrew philology
and a concern for the *Peshaṭ,* to the Jews of France and Italy.
In him the synthesis of traditional Judaism with the cultural
achievement of Muslim Spain culminates in a series of
original exegetical works, of which his commentary on the
Torah is perhaps the most important.

A separate commentary on Exodus is rich in grammatical
observations which reflect the influence of Sa'adya and
his successors. Commentaries on Isaiah and the Twelve
Prophets, on Psalms, Job, Esther, Ruth, the Song of Songs,
Ecclesiastes and Daniel, amply testify to his extensive knowledge of the religious and secular sciences, to his independent, sound judgment and to a rare insight into the
theological and ethical content of the Bible. His colourful
personality developed on journeys in Europe which also
brought him to England; it mirrors the richness of an
original mind which is open to the impressions of a varied,
mature civilisation. Its achievements are pressed into the
service of Judaism, which he spared no effort to explain to
his generation.

His innermost thoughts are often concealed in riddles,

hints and allusions; he is fond of speaking of secrets hidden in the commandments and the stories of the Bible. But he is explicit when dealing with the preceptive part of Scripture and he brings his vast learning and exegetical skill to bear on the literal meaning. His audacity in applying a literary criticism not unlike that of the modern critical approach to the Bible, to the Pentateuch and to Isaiah must, however, not mislead us into doubting his absolute loyalty to rabbinic Judaism or his acceptance of the *Torah* as Mosaic. But he claimed that some additions were made to the Pentateuch after Moses's death, and he implied that we must distinguish a Second Isaiah, though he is less explicit than Moses ibn Gikatilla whom he quotes.

He was essentially a mediaeval Jew and not a Higher Critic, at any rate in his clear statements. What he concealed in hints and allusions may be interpreted differently. But we should remember that he was a responsible spiritual leader of a community which had to fight for survival and did so fight with determination and courage assailed by doubters in its own midst and by Muslim and Christian hostility towards its faith and practice.

There is only one biblical book in expounding which he resorted to an allegorical meaning: the Song of Songs. In the introduction to his commentary, he states that a secret meaning is sealed in this most excellent of all the songs of Solomon. But he observed the rule of the rabbis that, although several meanings are permissible in addition to the literal meaning, they can never supplant the *Peshat*. Thus, he says that he wrote a threefold commentary on the Song of Songs: his first objective is to explain every obscure word; after this has been done, he explains the plain, simple meaning of its contents; and only in the third place does he employ the method of *derash*, as the rabbis had done before him.

What is his own method of interpretation? He sets it out
in the introduction to his commentary on the *Torah*; it
shows clearly the continuity of Jewish exegesis, its eminently
practical concern and its foremost aim, namely, to present
and maintain the *Torah* as "a fountain of living waters", as
"a tree of life" to sustain his contemporaries just as effectively
as it had previous generations of loyal Jews, and to hand on
a living legacy to future generations. His exegesis further
shows the application of the exegetical activity of Jewry
under Islam to their brothers under the much less tolerant
dominion of Christianity. Moreover, this application, thanks
to its scholarly method, furnished a sharp weapon for the
defence of Judaism which can be summed up in the word
Peshaṭ.

Abraham ibn Ezra speaks of four methods of Bible interpretation: the method of the geonim is marred by the
presence of unnecessary extraneous elements, but he pays
tribute to and often quotes with approval the commentaries
of Sa'adya, who was undoubtedly their peer. The method
of the Karaites is criticised on the grounds that by ignoring
accumulated tradition they block the way to a true understanding. In his view, traditional exegesis is of inestimable
help to the contemporary commentator. Next, he reviews
the method of Rashi and his French school of commentators
and finds that they pay too much attention to the *derash* of
midrashic literature and too little to the results of recent
linguistic studies and that they allow insufficient use of
critical reasoning. He himself employs the "method of
Midrash" only to point up the connection between passages
and chapters.

If we want to penetrate to the plain, literal meaning of the
Hebrew text we must strictly apply the laws of language and
of logic. This is his principal method and concern, and he,
therefore, flatly rejects the allegorising interpretation of the

Christian sages who, so he claims, allege that the whole *Torah*, including all the legal parts, consists of riddles and allegories. To the Christians, everything contains a hint, an allusion. He denounces their method—like David Kimchi after him—as vanity and hot air, rejects their typological Christological interpretation and insists that every commandment is to be understood as it is written. We said earlier that Ibn Ezra holds that there are secrets contained in the Bible, such as the tree of knowledge or paradise, which reason cannot explain. But he appeals to the intellect implanted in man by God, to demonstrate the *peshaṭ*. He tries in his own exegetical work to strike a fair balance between rational and traditional interpretation, relying mainly on language and logic.

PHILOSOPHICAL EXEGESIS

Rational interpretation bursts the limits of *peshaṭ* as soon as it takes into consideration not only language and logic, but also physics and metaphysics. The intellectual premises and aims of philosophical exegesis must be dealt with in the context of Muslim and Jewish religious philosophy which are the result of the confrontation with Greek and Hellenistic philosophy. At present, we are concerned only with the application of philosophical speculation to the Bible. Scholars differ widely as to the nature and import of the philosophical approach to the Bible in the Middle Ages. This is not the place to decide whether the starting point of our religious thinkers was Aristotle or the *Torah*, whether Aristotle confirmed the Bible or Scripture confirmed Aristotle, since truth is indivisible and, therefore, the Bible cannot contradict Aristotle or vice versa.

Suffice it to say that wherever the individual thinkers may

have stood, they all started from the axiom that the Bible was revealed truth and as such had to form the basis of their speculation. Philosophical truth established by demonstrative proof is in complete agreement with revealed truth, but it is neither as comprehensive nor as infallible, since human reason is limited. We recall how Sa'adya tried to balance reason with trustworthy tradition based on revelation.

His successors went to great lengths to square philosophical with scriptural truth by ascribing to a passage a figurative meaning which vitiated the literal meaning. Maimonides's *Guide* is largely philosophical interpretation of the Bible in an attempt to reconcile its doctrines with Aristotelian philosophy. In many instances the Aristotelian meaning assigned to the Bible can be obtained only if we ignore the *peshaṭ*. But to my mind, Maimonides was careful not to undermine the foundations of the *Torah* and to respect the fundamental teachings of Judaism. Thus, he accepted the Genesis story of the creation of the world out of nothing in its literal sense because Aristotle had not convinced him philosophically of the eternity of matter. Whether the traditionalist Maimonides would have made way for the metaphysician if Aristotle had proved his case and if he then had looked for a different basis for the *Torah* is an open question. It cannot be proved—we only have his own words in Book II, Chapter 25—but I doubt whether such a responsible leader of his generation would have risked moving the *Torah* from its authoritative position. It is possible that he would have abandoned the biblical principle and shifted the authority of the *Torah* and its eternal validity to the revelation on Sinai which is attested by the eye witness of the assembled Israelites. Fortunately, Aristotle did not force him to do so.

At any rate, Maimonides did not doubt the Divine character of the *Torah* any more than any believer in his day, and he would not abolish the least of the commandments since all were equally obligatory as divine revelation. He shared with rabbinic and earlier philosophical exegesis the rejection of anthropomorphism. Religious belief, not philosophical proof, forced him to explain away the bodily representation of God and to understand the relevant passages in a metaphorical sense. But when he identified the angels with Aristotle's separate intelligences he could hardly expect that the strict adherents of traditional exegesis would follow him. But in this point religious belief and philosophical conviction did not contradict each other: an angel is a disembodied spiritual substance, hence to identify him with a separate intelligence is quite legitimate. When it came to such basic religious concepts as providence and reward and punishment no metaphorical explanation was even attempted: these teachings were essential for any and every believer.

That a danger to Judaism was involved would be denied by no one who knows how strongly the Christian case against the Old Testament is based on its allegorical interpretation. As long as Judaism depends on the strict fulfilment of the commandments, any tampering with the literal meaning carries with it the danger of anti-nomianism, be it for philosophical or mystical reasons. The struggle that raged round Maimonides cannot be described here. David Kimchi's commentaries show his influence and those of Gersonides. Kimchi, one of Maimonides's staunchest defenders, gives many philosophical explanations in his commentaries, otherwise devoted to the *peshaṭ*, which have had such a great influence on Christian Hebraists. Gersonides has perfected the philosophical exegesis as a strict Aristotelian. This much is certain, that the rational explanation of those commandments which human reason could understand helped to strengthen the loyalty to their ancestral faith of those whose contact with contemporary philosophy had sown doubt and confusion in their minds.

In passing, it may be noticed that Maimonides exerted considerable influence on the pillars of the Medieval Church, the scholastics: Alexander of Hales, Albert the Great and especially Thomas Aquinas.

Sa'adya had borrowed from Muslim theology the division of the commandments into those of reason and those of revelation, which were both contained in the perfect *Torah*. Maimonides objected to this division and replaced it by that into judicial laws and ceremonial laws, the reasons for which man cannot establish rationally. In this point as in others he has influenced the scholastics. Thomas Aquinas is indebted to "R. Moyses" for the explanation of the sacrifices, circumcision, and Sabbath observance, contained in the third book of the *Guide*. We shall say a little more about their relationship when we discuss theology and philosophy later on.

MYSTICAL EXEGESIS

To round off this brief survey of biblical exegesis, reference ought at least to be made to mystical exegesis. This is, however, hardly possible or useful without an account of the origin and development of Jewish mysticism which I am unable to provide. The reader is referred to G. Sholem's authoritative *Major Trends in Jewish Mysticism*. The proper place for such a discussion would be in the section dealing with theology and philosophy, owing to the rationalist bias of the mystics and to the fact that Sa'adya has made a substantial contribution to mystical thought in Judaism by his development of *Merkavah*-mysticism. One aspect of mysticism will occupy us a little later: a certain ascetic tendency shared with Sufism.

Here it must suffice to recall that talmudic Judaism from the days of the Mishna onwards, had adherents of *gnosis* who indulged in mystical speculations. The famous Kalonymides, in touch with mystical Jewish circles in Iraq, brought mystical teachings from Italy to Germany and appear to have paved the way for the German *Chassidim*. At any rate, a mystical strand was added to biblical exegesis in the thirteenth century. Moses ben Nachman (Nachmanides), in his valuable commentary on the *Torah*, combined with the primary method of *peshaṭ* a mystical tendency, but mainly in hints and allusions. Only his disciple, Bachya ben Asher, to whom we referred earlier, introduced the mystical interpretation proper (*Kabbalah*) into his commentary (from 1291) alongside the three methods of *peshaṭ* (literal, historical, linguistic); *midrash* (metaphorical); *sechel* (intellect, rational-philosophical). He accepts the first two well-established methods unquestioningly, but makes reservations concerning the third which he only allows in so far as it agrees with the text and tradition. *Kabbalah* is the new element which he stresses and employs relying on earlier mystical works. The link with the *Zohar*, ascribed to Moses de Leon, cannot be pursued here. Bachya combines in his term *kabbalah* both *remez* and *sod*, allusion and mystery. Both terms correspond to the Christian methods of *allegoria* and *anagogia*, the typological and mystical interpretation of Scripture.

In conclusion it can be stated that all types of exegesis, singly and combined, aimed at an interpretation of the Hebrew Bible designed to show the relevance and significance of the Book of Divine Revelation for their generation whose adherence to the *Torah* and to Tradition through the conscientious and willing fulfilment of the *mitsvot* was to enable them to know and love God.

SCIENCE AND MEDICINE

One of the many lasting contributions which Islam has made to what we generally call 'Western Civilisation' is the creative transmission of Greek science and philsophy. It is true that science and medicine have not affected Muslim thought in the same way as philosophy. But they cannot be kept separate as being of no consequence for the religious foundation and direction of Islamic culture. For they stem from the same rational quest for truth and knowledge as do the philosophical sciences. The world view of Muslims and Jews was strongly influenced by their knowledge of the physical universe; their way of life was determined by their technical knowledge and ability, and what we call civilisation in contradistinction from (spiritual) culture is largely dependent on their knowledge of geometry, mechanics, optics, astronomy and the like. The Arabs transmitted to Europe an extensive knowledge of Greek medicine and pharmacology. Arab medicine was entirely built on Greek foundations and attained a high standard of medical theory and practice. This was facilitated in the first place by Arabic translations of Greek medical writings, but the Arab contribution to medical knowledge consists in much more than mere transmission; by study and observation, Arab and Jewish physicians were able to add to the store of past knowledge and to extend the frontiers of medicine and pharmacology to climes and regions which were beyond the reach of their Greek masters.

The Jews have their full share in this transmission. Not only did they supply many eminent physicians and medical writers of distinction, they also furnished experts in astronomy and astrology ('practical astronomy') and in mathematics, as writers in their own right and as translators. The reader must be referred to the vast literature on the subject, especially to the unsurpassed M. Steinschneider's many studies and his monumental *Hebrew translations of the Middle Ages* (in German). Astronomy was, of course, a necessary auxiliary science for the vital fixing of the calendar, and we find Maimonides fully conversant with it in the third book of his Code, the "Book of the Seasons" in ten treatises. Ptolemy's important *Almagest* was translated from Arabic into Hebrew at an early date and Jews had a large share in making this basic work available in Latin to the Christian West.

Of medical writers, we need mention only Isaac Israeli and Maimonides and the Hebrew translation of Avicenna's *Canon of Medicine*, an encyclopedia of medicine based mainly on Galen, but containing many original observations of Avicenna who was himself an eminent physician. It was translated into Latin by Gerard of Cremona, a prolific translator, ably assisted in Toledo by a Christian and a Jew, and remained a standard work in Europe right into the seventeenth century. He surpasses Avendeath (Ibn Da'ud), a Jewish convert to Christianity, a native of Toledo, known as Johannes Hispalensis, who translated from Arabic and Hebrew into Latin. Of particular interest in our context is Maimonides's medical legacy. Like Isaac Israeli in Kairouan, whom he praised as a physician but did not think much of as a philosopher, he was court physician under Saladin and his sons in Cairo. His best known medical work is entitled *Aphorisms* and in it he dared to criticise Galen. He also wrote for his masters many treatises on hygiene.

These few examples may suffice to indicate all too briefly and sketchily the share which the Jews have in the dissemination of scientific and medical knowledge throughout the far flung Muslim empire and beyond, especially in the Latin West through the translations made in Spain either directly from Arabic into Latin or first into Hebrew and or Spanish. In this field, there existed harmonious co-operation between Muslims, Jews and Christians in the interest of science and learning.

That the spirit of inquiry and of experiment should leave its mark on the more strictly religious sciences like biblical exegesis, *Halachah* and theology is only natural. Living in an environment in which belief in authority was a matter of course, it can be readily imagined that, although not un-critical even towards such authorities as Ptolemy and Galen, Aristotle and Plato and their commentators and successors, a challenge of enormous power had to be met. The faith of these scholars was certainly put to a severe test. For even if their own powers of observation made them question certain details of the system inherited from classical antiquity, by and large the authority of the ancient philosophers was firmly established and acknowledged. This respect for the authority resting in writings effectively separates the 'scholars' of the Middle Ages from modern scholarship, which knows no authority but reason and experiment and which must subject tradition to the acid test of these two authorities. Whether science and learning are in fact so objective is another matter: we are concerned only with the ideal demand at the moment.

In judging the achievement of medieval man—Jew, Christian and Muslim alike—we must therefore see things in their proper perspective. Then we shall find that there is a fundamental difference in approach and attitude between the Middle Ages and the modern age, though many of the questions agitating our minds are eternal and were their questions as well. The reason why the solutions or the answer cannot, however, simply be transferred from them to us lies mainly in our different attitude to authority, the authority of religion and the authority of science.

THEOLOGY AND PHILOSOPHY

THE PROBLEM

If we see the challenge to Islam of Greek and Hellenistic philosophy as the challenge of an authority based on human reason to the authority of Scripture, the result of Divine Revelation, the problem is by far the most vital question of the Middle Ages in the realm of the spirit. For Judaism the challenge was not a new one; it had to face it in the period of Hellenism, and Philo of Alexandria had boldly taken up the challenge in the first half of the first century C.E. and met it by drawing a distinction between the law of God, the divinely revealed *Torah*, and the law of human reason, the *Nomos* of the Greeks. This distinction is absolutely fundamental and thanks to it the Middle Ages were able to assimilate as much of Greek-Hellenistic philosophy as could be accommodated to the religious system based on the superior law.

It is remarkable that Philo could grasp the difference so clearly and could determine the rôle of philosophy in Judaism so decisively, since he lived outside the mainstream of Jewish thought working for and steadily developing "the fence round the *Torah*" by evolving the *Halachah*. That Philo could do this shows not only the close link between the Greek-speaking Jewish Diaspora and *Erets Yisrael*, but also—and this is of immense importance—that from the beginning of the historical encounter between *Torah*-culture and the sophisticated Greek culture centred in rational man, the Jew took his stand on Revelation in the form of prophetic law. For whether Philo directly influenced medieval Jewish thought or not, his reaction to the challenge of philosophy—a philosophy which in its Hellenistic form tended towards a religious monism—was basically the same as that of our medieval religious thinkers.

They were in many ways better prepared for the on-slaught than their Muslim masters who transmitted that philosophy to them. For they had developed a mature way of life centred in the *Torah* as *Halachah* which was able to withstand the shock of the rationalist *critique* and scepticism of their Islamic environment. This scepticism is the direct result of the spread of Greek-Hellenistic thought in Arabic translations which stimulated theological controversy in an atmosphere strongly influenced by the comparative study of religions. One could say that the defensive armour of the Jews was donned well in advance of the attack. That the attack was serious and was recognised as such is evidenced by the fact that the outstanding intellect among tenth century Jewry, Sa'adya Gaon, had to speak and write in defence of Judaism. In so doing he inaugurated Jewish religious philosophy, though he was anticipated in philoso-phical studies by his older contemporaries Isaac Israeli and David al-Muqammis.

RELIGIOUS PHILOSOPHY

Theology and philosophy cannot be kept strictly separate, for it would be superficial, if not actually wrong, to draw a line between the heavens which are the realm of meta-physics and theology and the sub-lunar sphere which is the realm of physics. The only justification for such a division could be seen in the fact that religious philosophy actually delimits the sphere of influence or of authority in this way: what is under the heavens is explained by Aristotle, what is in the heavens is looked after by the *Torah*. This subdivision is, however, of paramount importance in that it precludes,

from the outset, an independent philosophy, that is, a rational
inquiry without premises, an 'objective' search for truth
unaided by divine revelation. Neither Islamic nor Jewish
medieval philosophy is pure philosophy. The fact that we
meet with large-scale acceptance of Aristotelian and Neo-
Platonic philosophy in certain branches and the use of
philosophical argument and demonstrative proof in theology
does not invalidate this claim.

For Jewish religious philosophy starts from theological
presuppositions. At the beginning and in the centre of
philosophical speculation stands the One God whose existence is assumed and has to be proved philosophically
although it is attested by revelation in history. In fact the
proof from history—revelation from Sinai in the presence
of the children of Israel—takes precedence over the onto-
logical and teleological proofs. In other words, religious
doctrine precedes philosophical speculation, determines its
course and limits its scope. Hence, we can only speak of
religious philosophy. This means in the first place that insofar as it starts from God it is both theology and philosophy.
Its philosophical argument proves His existence and Oneness and absolute Unity, and it leads to God. The twin aim
of philosophy—self-knowledge and self-fulfilment in attain-
ing the Highest Good—is also its aim. But it relates human
happiness to God and makes its fulfilment dependent on
man's serving God in knowledge and in love. Man is still
God's most important creation, His most favoured one, because he is gifted with reason. He has been given reason to
use it: hence the justification—on religious grounds—of
philosophy. But the ultimate object of his rational inquiry
is God: he must find God in his thought and in his action.
Knowledge of God, even knowledge of the *Torah* as the
guide to Him, can best be acquired with the help of philosophy. In this sense, Philo has already stated that philosophy

G

is the handmaid of wisdom, by which he means the *Torah*.
But philosophy as the search for truth, for wisdom, is not
only concerned with the justification of faith on rational
grounds; it is itself justified by the commandment of the
Torah to acquire knowledge by study. Thus the intellectualism of the medieval thinkers derived the duty to philosophical speculation from revelation. Demonstrative argument
was the supreme means for confirming the truth of
revelation.

While, as stated before, the borderline between theology
and philosophy is fluid and often blurred, religious philosophy is only akin to, but by no means identical with, theology. That they are two separate disciplines is clear from the
difference of the questions which they ask and the way in
which they choose to answer and solve them.

Even though the ultimate object of medieval philosophy
is, to repeat, the knowledge of God, this object is reached
by acquiring a knowledge and understanding of the Universe first. To understand Reality created by God means to
experience God in His oneness and unity. The religious
thinker knows that God exists and that, in the words of Job,
"my redeemer liveth". The *Torah* tells him so and commands him to believe it. He not only wants but is obliged
to obtain this knowledge because the *Torah* commands him
to know. Philosophy is thus a way to God, not the only one,
but the way appropriate to the philosopher. It cannot and
must not take the place of the fulfilment of the *mitsvot*: the
philosopher does not stand above the Law but lives under
it; he must fulfil the *Torah* just as every naive, simple believer must do. While all believers are equal in the sight of
God, the philosopher's intelligent belief is superior to that
of the pious soul who simply obeys the will of God by ob-
serving the *Halachah*. The difference, seen from the point of
view of religion, is one of degree, not of substance. A prob-

lem arises—and with it the possibility of conflict—only when the philosopher in his search for truth studies the strictly philosophical disciplines which the Greeks called theoretical philosophy—physics and metaphysics, which have no direct relationship with religion in contrast to logic and mathematics. Metaphysics, as its name implies, goes beyond the physical world. Did we not say that the heavens belong to God? What business has man, then, to probe the celestial spheres, to eat of the forbidden fruit? Here lies the crux of the matter, and the Jew who lived within the four ells of the *Halachah* considered the philosopher's audacity wrong and dangerous. The religious thinker admitted the limitations of reason, but did not accept the narrow limits the pure traditionalist wanted to impose on rational inquiry. The philosopher claimed the right and the duty to investigate everything which was within reach of human reason. He would not stop at the physical world in the strict sense of the term. For does the earth not belong to God as much as the heavens? The more extensive, the more profound man's knowledge of the working of God's creation was the more firmly established his reverent faith in God would be. And yet, the medieval thinkers felt that the difficulty was a real one and they took it upon themselves to aim at a synthesis of faith and reason, at a reconciliation between religion and philosophy. There is only one truth: religion and philosophy, revelation and reason teach the same truth, but in different ways. The aim of both is the same, but the road leading to the end is different.

TRANSMISSION

This can best be seen in what the Greeks called Practical Philosophy, that is Ethics, Politics and Economics. It is represented by such Greek works as Plato's *Republic* and *Laws* and Aristotle's *Nicomachean Ethics*. It found its way to the Jews via the Muslims. This is important because Greek philosophy did not filter through to Judaism in its pure authentic form, but had undergone a certain transformation and adaptation to Muslim monotheism. The actual route of transmission with the problems it set to translators, who had to coin a philosophical terminology first, does not concern us here. But we would do well to remember that Hebrew literature and its language essentially lacked the abstract terms of philosophical speculation even more than Arabic on which of necessity it modelled itself. The basic similarity between the two Semitic languages helped the Jewish translators to adapt this philosophical vocabulary to rabbinic Hebrew. However, this similarity is to some extent responsible for a not inconsiderable number of errors and inaccuracies which have crept into the Hebrew translations even more than into the Arabic. For the Hebrew translator often used the same Hebrew root although its meaning differed from the Arabic. This is bad enough in translations from the Arabic original, it is worse in translations into Hebrew from an Arabic which is itself a translation either directly from the Greek or from a Syriac version of the Greek original. Though allowance must be made for this source of error and misunderstanding, enough genuine Greek thought has been transmitted and transformed to enable us to gauge the influence of Greek ideas on indigenous Jewish concepts. As we know, the meeting between revelation and reason did not stop with Practical Philosophy, it also extended to Theoretical Philosophy and it included the very concept of God. This is not surprising since there is only one *philosophy* and its division into two parts is more a matter of method than of substance: both parts belong together and complement each other. To take one obvious example: the purpose of politics is to attain the highest good or happiness. Politics is the science that leads to this aim; but the aim itself is—insofar as it is a truly human aim—a higher good, be it *theoria*, contemplation, or *praxis*, good deeds, action, or both together.

That practical philosophy as such should appeal to Muslims and Jews is natural; it did not conflict with the ethical concepts and demands of their monotheism. But how can we account for the entry of metaphysics into both religions when we know that, as Yehuda Halevi so aptly put it: "The God of Abraham is not the god of Aristotle"? Did not Abraham ibn Da'ud, the wrongly neglected precursor of Maimonides, say in the introduction to his *Exalted Faith*: "It happens occasionally in our time that he who studies the sciences a little has no power to hold two candles in his two hands, the light of his faith in his right hand and the light of his wisdom in his left. For when the light of philosophy is kindled, the light of religion goes out"? This real difficulty led Sa'adya in the ninth century in Babylonia, Abraham ibn Da'ud and Maimonides in the twelfth century in Spain to write their philosophical treatises to bridge the gap and to put a stop to confusion and doubt.

COMMON GROUND AND CONTRAST

How did they find the means for a reconciliation, how could they reconcile religion and philosophy? The answer is not only interesting because it shows how two basically different cultures, different in origin, intention and in end, could be brought to a successful merger—up to a point; it is also important in that it shows what the two cultures have in common and in what they radically differ.

What, then, is this common ground between Hellas and

Islam and Judaism? It is the concept of law and of State and society based on law. Justice is the primary virtue in the city-State of Plato as well as in the community of the faithful and in the Congregation of Israel. Justice is first and foremost a political virtue second only to wisdom, which cannot flourish without it. On the sure foundation of law and justice it was possible for the Jewish thinkers to bring the Greek and Jewish concepts of God, which are otherwise so utterly irreconcilable, closer to one another, or at any rate close enough to apply the methods and concepts of metaphysics to the *Torah*. For Plato's God shares with the God of Islam and of Israel the attribute of justice. But here the parallel ends, and it must be plain that the self-thinking thought of Aristotle or even the demiurge of Plato are not identical with the God of creation who has created His world out of love and for the good of man whom He has fashioned in His image.

This fundamental difference also illuminates what I said earlier on about the theological presuppositions with which Muslims and Jews entered upon their philosophical speculation. For a number of important religious beliefs and convictions follow from the concept of the God of the Bible. They are Prophecy, Sin and Atonement, Reward and Punishment, Providence and Messianism. Here, a warning is necessary. When we read Maimonides and Gersonides we realise that they, in common with Al-Fārābī and Avicenna, the principal Muslim teachers of the medieval Jewish thinkers, identify the personal God of the Bible with "the first cause", "the first mover" or "world reason", that is the God of medieval Aristotelianism modified by Neo-Platonism. Some thinkers, for instance Isaac Israeli and Ibn Gabirol (in his *Fountain of Life*), are much nearer to "the One" of Plotinus. In fact, it was the religious monism of the Neo-Platonists mediated to the Muslims through the so-called *Theology of Aristotle*—an extract from Plotinus' *Enneads* with its theory of emanation—which next to the common ground of law and justice made the reception of Platonic and Aristotelian ideas in Islam and from it in Judaism possible. This Neo-platonic monism helped Greek philosophy to be welcomed into the ethical montheism of medieval Islam and Judaism. It also helped to confuse the issue by its use of such religious concepts as the "imitation of God" and love and providence, to name only a few. This raises an important question, hence the warning. How do we know what these terms mean when used by mono-theistic thinkers? Do they use them in their Islamic or Jewish connotation or in their philosophical, intellectual meaning? Do Al-Fārābī, Avicenna, Averroes and their Jewish disciples and contemporaries use the term "World to come" or "Hereafter" in the scriptural or in the philosophical sense? In some cases these questions can be solved, in others there remains a doubt. Much depends on our interpretation and here much depends on how we read the texts: do we accept them at their face value or do we read between the lines? Which method of interpretation do we adopt: the *peshaṭ* or the *derash*? Do the authors mean what they say or do they intend an inner esoteric meaning? Were they actually sincere believers or did they only pay lip-service to save their skins at a time—the twelfth century in Almohad Spain, for ex-ample—when heresy hunting was the order of the day and when to conform meant to live in peace? To my mind, the issue is not quite so clear-cut. For the very existence of inconsistencies and contradictions—especially in Maimon-ides, if I understand him aright—points to sincerity of belief no less than of practice. Religion and philosophy have much in common, but they "live" on two different levels of consciousness which human weakness cannot always keep strictly apart. Faith is an act of will; once we have made that decision and believe we are no longer the same person as before. Certain beliefs and convictions become axiomatic with us, that is, they are, while still accessible to rational argument, no longer dependent on rational affirmation by demonstrative proof.

This is precisely the position of men like Maimonides and Averroes: they exclude certain concepts and phenomena from rational inquiry; they accept them as axiomatic because they are commanded by revelation. Avicenna is fundamentally in the same position, with this difference, however, that his mysticism blurred the issue in that it resolved the contradiction; it overcame the tension by the intuitive perception of God in the act of mystical contemplation.

Finally, we note that the common ground of law and justice at the same time points to the fundamental distinction which our religious thinkers have drawn between the *Torah* as the law of God revealed through Moses the greatest of all prophets, and the *Nomos*, the man-made law of the philosopher-king of the Greek city-State. The Divine law is perfect; it is superior to the human law which must needs be less comprehensive and less perfect as the result of fallible human reason. This premise is an axiom with all mediaeval thinkers and it provides the clearest indication of the scale of values they adopt: authority belongs to the *Torah* of Moses, "the man of God"; its authority overrides that of the *Nomos* of the Greeks which, in the words of Maimonides, is a political law that guarantees the welfare of the body. The Divine *Torah* cares for the welfare of the body *and* of the soul; it guarantees man's twofold happiness in this world and the next.

BELIEFS AND CONVICTIONS

The scene is now set for a more detailed description of the influence of Greek on Jewish medieval thought, mediated to the religious thinkers of Judaism by those of Islam.

We begin with the concept of God. Proceeding chronologically, we should first deal with Sa'adya. But lack of space allows us only a passing reference. In our discussion of Jewish Law, we noted that Maimonides rejected the division of the law made by Sa'adya into laws of revelation and laws of reason. Maimonides accuses the Gaon of following the *Kalam*, the dialectic theology of Islam. Sa'adya in fact adopted contemporary Mu'tazilite theories. The *Mu'tazila* is the rationalist wing of what became later—under the spiritual leadership of Al-Ash'ari—'orthodox' theology, with less emphasis on reason. But the Mu'tazilite theologians did much to purify the concept of God in their strict adherence to the concept of the absolute unity of God and in their interpretation of His attributes. They fought strenuously against anthropomorphic notions of God.

Now Sa'adya starts from the creation out of nothing, which demands One Creator from outside. Next, he establishes the unity of God; then he postulates that the three attributes of the Creator-God—life, power and wisdom—are implied in His essence. Sa'adya means by this assumption that these three attributes are not attributes of essence at all, but simply point to the existence of the creation. Maimonides later called the attributes those of action, which is not quite the same thing, since Sa'adya uses them only in relation to something outside God.

Maimonides's concept of God marks a distinct advance: thanks to his deeper understanding of Aristotle, helped by Al-Fārābī and Avicenna, his argument is more cogent and

systematic. He is concerned—in common with all philosophers of the period—with the existence, unity and incor-
poreality of God which he sets out to prove in twenty-five
propositions with which he introduces the second book of
his *Guide*. Maimonides insists, against Aristotle, as already
mentioned, upon the creation out of nothing as the outcome
of God's Free Will. Some of his propositions were correctly
traced to Avicenna, among them the view that in God
existence and essence are one, whilst in His creatures existence is an accident superimposed on their essence. Avicenna's
importance for Jewish philosophy consists in the first place
in his view that in God as the necessary Being essence and
existence are identical, that He is not subject to change, is
immaterial, is not the Prime Mover but the Prime Cause and
the Creator of the whole creation. I cannot here discuss in
detail the impact of this concept, both positively and
negatively, on Jewish thinkers, especially on Maimonides
who, in any case, valued Al-Fārābī much more highly as
a philosopher.

An important pointer to the attitude of theologians and
philosophers to philosophy and to their view of the mutual
relationship between philosophy and revelation is their
method of presentation and argument. Thus, Saʿadya states
in his *Beliefs and Convictions*, in justifying knowledge of
reason in addition to knowledge through sense perception,
that our starting point must be revelation: God informs us
through His prophets about His oneness, power and wisdom.
Why do we accept this information? Because the prophets
confirm their God-inspired statements by signs and miracles.
After that acceptance, we test what revelation and sense perception have compelled us to accept with our reasoning
faculty, and come to the same result. That means, Reason
verifies Revelation. At times, for instance in the question of
Divine Attributes, Saʿadya went back to Scripture for

renewed confirmation of the agreement between Reason and Revelation.

It will be seen from this method that religious philosophy is closely linked to the Bible and that it is actually rational exegesis of it. To repeat, because it is so important, Scripture cannot say what runs counter to Reason. If Scripture contains statements which cannot be verified by Reason they must be interpreted in such a way that agreement is reached, provided tradition bears out such an interpretation. Apart from this, there are commandments which are beyond the grasp of Reason; since they are revealed we must accept them. Thus, Revelation takes precedence over Reason.

So much for the philosophical justification and confirmation of Scripture in relation to the concept of God. That there was determined opposition to this rational probing with its departure from the literal meaning has already been mentioned. This opposition was not confined to those who denied the philosophical sciences any entry altogether into Judaism and its exposition.

YEHUDA HALEVI

Religious thinkers with a philosophical bent like Yehuda Halevi likewise deprecated strongly the suggestion that the truth of revelation should be subjected to the scrutiny of fallible human reason. Halevi was certainly well versed in philosophy as the reader of his *Kuzari*: "Book of Proof and Argument in Defence of a Despised Religion" soon realises. Philosophy was part of his mental make-up and he used the philosophical method skilfully. In this, he resembles Ghazali among the Muslims whose attack on philosophy has forced subsequent Muslim thinkers, chief among them Averroes (Ibn Rushd), on to the defensive. Halevi, like

Ghazali, allowed logic and mathematics as branches of theoretical philosophy, but warned against physics and metaphysics. Practical philosophy was well within the bounds of permissibility, and Halevi appreciates what human reason can do with its help: law and order in the State, social justice and a sound economy are due to the philosophical sciences of politics, ethics and economics.

But in the realm of religion Halevi strenuously opposes the speculative theories of the philosophers. They lack certainty and only confuse. Revelation is not only sufficient, but superior and by far preferable, since it provides well attested historical facts. God's revelation to the patriarchs, the Exodus from Egypt, the revelation of the *Torah* to Moses at Sinai are all attested through experience and through uninterrupted, trustworthy tradition. They vouchsafe to the believer that certainty which his reason is unable to give him. Prophets who announce God's revelation and priests who teach and guard the *Torah* guarantee the truth of revelation and enable the pious to lead a life of faith, piety and good deeds. Religious experience, feeling and conviction determine religious life, not speculation and philosophical argument. The spontaneity of faith of the pious soul counted most; it sustained the individual Jew and kept the community of Israel alive.

Abraham ibn Da'ud and Maimonides, and even Sa'adya before them, did not think so. For they were sure that in order to understand the bases of our faith we must thoroughly study the secular philosophical disciplines; a knowledge of physics and metaphysics is essential for the perception of Reality and its divine Creator. Demonstrative proof must supplement the proof of Revelation contained in Scripture. This means, at the same time, that the truth of philosophy is contained in the Bible, but not in the form of demonstrative argument. On that basis, the religious thinker is not only permitted, but is actually obliged to prove the existence of God with the arguments of Aristotle. Abraham ibn Da'ud died a martyr's death in 1180; Maimonides, born in Cordova in 1135, died in Cairo in 1204. Yehuda Halevi had not convinced them that philosophy was inadequate, that it could not inspire its adherents with the desire to love the personal God of the Bible which they no less considered to be the highest aim of man.

Yehuda Halevi expressed the contrast between the God of Israel and the God of Aristotle in a striking interpretation of the two Divine names *Elohim* (God) and *Adonai* (the Lord) used in the Bible. "The Lord" is a personal God whom we know through prophecy. On the other hand, "God" can be understood by every rational human being. For does not human reason come to the conclusion that the world is in need of One who orders and rules it? That is *Elohim*. But *Adonai* reveals Himself only to the prophets of Israel, the most perfect of human beings, whose souls are translucent so that the Divine light can penetrate them as the light of the sun shines through the crystal. Yehuda Halevi adduces scriptural evidence to show that this Divine light raises the prophet among the angels and separates him from his ordinary human fellows. He experiences "The Lord" without logical proof; his desire is for Him whom he serves in love. He is prepared to lay down his life in the service of the Lord. The philosopher, on the other hand, draws near to "God" through speculation; he worships truth; he is not willing to suffer for his religion of reason. The steel of reason is not one of the constituent elements of a living faith for our eloquent and profound poet.

The truth of Judaism is proved by the historical fact that *Adonai* has revealed Himself from Sinai to the whole people of Israel assembled at the foot of the holy mountain; He has bound them to Himself by His perfect Law.

PROPHECY

To return to Maimonides and his predecessors and successors; the duty of philosophical affirmation and confirmation of the truth of revelation in no way diminished their
fervent belief and their enthusiasm. Their acquaintance with
the philosophy of Plato in particular had sharpened their
perception that Judaism as a way of life—not only for the
metaphysician but for the whole people of Israel—was the
supreme example of the ideal State, superior to that of
Plato's *Republic* and *Laws* as the *Torah* must be superior to
the *Nomos*. The *Torah* was the ideal constitution, but it was
not to remain an ideal to which man might by great effort
approximate without ever reaching it. It was to be realised
at the end of days when God will raise His Messiah of the
house of king David. The *Torah* was not only a guide like
Plato's constitution devised and implemented by the
philosopher-king, though it was this too; through its Divine
origin and promulgation it was the perfect guide to man's
happiness which, as we stated above, consisted in the perception and love of God. For the *Torah* and it alone—to
quote from the *Guide*—aims at the best order of body and
faith alike. Its whole legislation for the individual and for
society is crowned by its teaching of right beliefs and sound
convictions about God and the angels, and about *Existing
Things*, that is Reality. This is a Platonic demand, the necessary foundation of the ideal State and the prerequisite for its
proper functioning. The philosophical preoccupation of
Maimonides is clear from his formulation of this foremost
aim of the *Torah*: "The *Torah* has given us the most important of the true ideas through which we reach ultimate
perfection and called upon us to believe in them in general,
that is in the existence of God, His unity, knowledge, power,

free will and eternity, which we can understand only after a careful study of other notions, belief in which is necessary for the best order of the State." We see from this statement firstly the religious foundation of the polity. Next, we note the stress on careful study of "other notions" which are essential for the functioning of the ideal State. No doubt, philsophy has to supply this knowledge, and metaphysics helps us to grasp the nature of God by giving us an understanding of His attributes of action, as far as the human intellect can comprehend it. But this is not all: for the *Torah* and it alone leads man to his destiny, which Maimonides in another passage in his *Guide* defines as "the imitation of God", by imitating His ways through the performance of the *mitsvot*. In other words, the science of politics, whose aim is man's Highest Good, is best taught in the *Torah*, the outcome of God's wisdom.

To understand this fully, it is necessary to discuss briefly Maimonides's concept of prophecy which leads us to inquire into its antecedents in Muslim philosophy, which is based on the practical philosophy of the Greeks.

PLATONISM IN ISLAM

It must suffice for our purpose to point to a few salient features of the philosophy of Al-Fārābī and Avicenna insofar as they have influenced Abraham ibn Da'ud and particularly Maimonides. We shall, then, see how in Maimonides's political interpretation of the *Torah* as the divine constitution of the ideal Jewish State acquaintance with Plato's political thought as mediated to him by Al-Fārābī and Avicenna has played a decisive part.

It is worthy of note that there is complete unity and agreement between Maimonides the disciple of Plato and

Maimonides the Halachist and spiritual leader of Jewry under Islam (strictly speaking only of Egyptian Jewry, but as we know from his letters his writ ran much further afield as well, including places as far as southern France).

Avicenna treats of prophecy in the last part of his *Metaphysics* which is, at a first glance surprisingly, devoted to Practical Philosophy. Abraham ibn Da'ud likewise concludes his *Exalted Faith* with a summary of Practical Philosophy, consisting of Politics, Ethics and Economics. This division goes back to Aristotle and must have come into Judaism through Avicenna. Al-Fārābī's *Encyclopedia* of the sciences seems to have stimulated Avicenna's treatise on *The Divisions of the Sciences*, from which we learn the reason why prophecy is included in Practical Philosophy. For, according to the Muslim thinkers prophecy is a natural, psychological phenomenon. Moreover, Avicenna states that prophecy and *Sharī'a* (which is linked to it through its two principal roots: Koran and *Sunna*, as we know) are necessary for mankind. This political motivation of prophecy is already fully developed by Al-Fārābī (died 950) in two political treatises which are based on Plato's *Republic* and *Laws*. Put in simple terms, the theory of prophecy is this: Man is endowed with theoretical and practical reason, that is, with imaginative and rational faculties, which are potentialities until they are actualised by the emanation of the Active Intellect. This Active Intellect is identified by the Muslim philosophers with the "Holy Spirit" or the angel Gabriel. (Here we have an interesting parallel with Jewish philosophical exegesis.) A man becomes a prophet if the outpouring from the Active Intellect first makes him into a philosopher by influencing his intellect and then impresses his imagination to the point of perfection. This perfect man, the prophet-philosopher, is the leader capable of guaranteeing law and order in society in which man must organise himself since he is, in the words of Aristotle, a political being, a citizen. Al-Fārābī thus adds the king to the prophetic lawgiver and philosopher and assimilates Plato's philosopher-king as the lawgiver to Islam by adding the necessary prophetic qualification. Necessary for what purpose? In order to enable man to reach his Highest Good: the rational perception of God.

Avicenna extends the prophetic qualities just described to comprise the working of miracles and spontaneous perception, intuitive knowledge through which the prophet surpasses the philosopher whose perception is dependent on study, on intellectual effort, on the use of demonstrative argument.

In his account of prophecy as a psychological state, Maimonides combines elements of both Muslim thinkers. But he makes several modifications, some formal, some substantial. While Al-Fārābī distinguishes only philosopher and prophet, Maimonides speaks of three classes which are determined by the effect of emanation on either their imaginative faculty alone—political leaders and lawgivers—or their rational faculty alone—philosophers—or on both together—the prophets. The prophet has reached highest human perfection; the lawgiver is superior to the political leader. This formal modification is of less significance than Maimonides's explicit divine veto: God can prevent prophecy materialising in a person naturally predisposed and qualified for it through the twofold emanation. Interestingly, Abraham ibn Da'ud had already expressed this opinion that God can, if He so wills, withhold the gift of prophecy and he backs it up with evidence from the Bible. Both Jewish thinkers safeguard God's free will and thus His power over nature. This agrees with Maimonides's attitude to miracles which, though akin to that of Moses ibn Gikatilla, explicitly upholds God's power to break through the natural laws governing the universe if He so wills, as He did, for example, at the passage of the Children of Israel through the Red Sea and, above all, at the Revelation from Sinai.

But of still greater significance is another modification made by Maimonides to the Muslim philosophers' theory of prophecy: he deliberately excludes Moses from the class of prophets whose prophethood has just been explained as a natural phenomenon. All other prophets have heard the voice of God or seen His angels, have had visions and dreams. Moses alone came face to face with God in direct communion, awake and composed. He alone was charged with the promulgation of the divine *Torah* and was commanded to lead and teach the people of Israel under the covenant between God who sent him and the people to whom he was sent. Avicenna and Averroes consider Mohammed in the same light: he, too, was sent to mankind with the divine law to preserve humanity in accordance with the will of God. As Maimonides puts it in his *Guide*: "the true law is unique, there is no other. It is the law of our master Moses ... to bring us the twofold perfection (of body and soul, of body and faith)."

THE PROPHECY OF MOSES

Let us look a little more closely at the special rôle assigned to Moses by Maimonides. Prophecy as explained by Al-Fārābī is derived from the Greeks. It has its origin either in middle Platonism or in the *Stoa*. No believer, Jew or Muslim, if he wants to conform to his indigenous tradition, can vindicate the Divine law as the perfect law superior to the man-made *Nomos* on the basis of a psychological theory. It is true that Al-Fārābī added the element of prophecy to Plato's philosopher-lawgiver-king. But Avicenna placed the prophet above the philosopher, and Averroes exempted Mohammed from the class of natural prophets and held fast to the traditional Muslim concept of *tanzīl*, of the sending down of the Koran.

Maimonides had a twofold aim in assigning Moses an exceptional status. As we saw, he distinguished the promulgator of the Divine law—as an apostle, a messenger, so-to-speak— from the natural prophecy of other prophets, in much the same way as his Muslim contemporary Averroes did with Mohammed. Moreover, he refused to recognise Mohammed's claim not only to prophecy, but to being the "seal of the prophets" by his emphasis on the uniqueness and exclusive authority of the Law of Moses, as is clear from the quotation given above. What grounds has he to deny Mohammed true prophetic status? To begin with, Maimonides stipulates not only intellectual, but also ethical perfection in the prophet. In this, he agrees with his Muslim teachers who, moreover, see in the legislative function the hallmark of the prophet. It is possible that Maimonides did not accept Al-Fārābi's identification of the prophetic lawgiver with Plato's philosopher-king for two reasons. In the first place, Judaism acknowledges the kingship of *Adonai* and sees in Moses not so much the lawgiver as the announcer of the law given by God. Moreover, the messianic king for whose coming Maimonides and all his generation eagerly waited, as we know from a famous letter and from his *Code*, was not identical with Moses, but was of the house of David. Secondly, Mohammed could not be accepted as falling into the same category as Moses. For this reason, Maimonides took exception to Mohammed even as a natural prophet in contrast to the one sent with the divine law by God. For he explicitly states in his *Guide* that sensuality, the satisfaction of the sexual impulse, renders a person unfit for prophecy. His commentators soon saw that this is directed against

Mohammed. That Maimonides could not openly say so is obvious. Hence he quotes Aristotle in support of his view and corroborates it with passages from Scripture.

Another shaft directed against Mohammed can be detected in Maimonides's differentiation between three kinds of law. The perfect law is sent by God through the prophet. The second law is a positive, human law, laid down by a statesman. The third law is a mixed law, half-prophetic, half-human positive. Mohammed's law is such a law since his claim to the Divine law cannot be accepted: as we know, there is only one Divine law, the law of our teacher Moses. The third law is falsely claimed to be inspired, prophetically received.

HAPPINESS

From the foregoing it should be clear that there is a close connection between prophecy and law. A further connection between both and the Highest Good or Happiness must now be discussed.

We recall that the aim of the science of politics has been defined by Aristotle as the Highest Good. Just as politics is a Greek science, so its aim is a Greek concept. Neither Islam nor Judaism have a term for it any more than they have for 'citizen'. The terms are borrowed from the Greek. This is not the place to give even a brief account of the meaning and development of the Greek idea of happiness or perfection. We have already heard that it is either knowledge or action or both. Muslims and Jews have taken it over in its twofold meaning, placing the emphasis now on theory now on practice, on contemplation or on good deeds. The ideal is perfection in ethical and intellectual virtues.

We had best confine our attention to Maimonides: he has defined it as the perception and love of God, as is commonly done in medieval Jewish philosophy from Sa'adya to Crescas and Albo. Love of God is understood by Sa'adya predominantly as intellectual love, a love springing from the knowledge and perception of God. In principle this is also the view of Leone Ebreo, the son of Don Isaac Abravanel, and of Spinoza. The differences do not concern us here.

There is no law which secures the attainment of the human aim, the fulfilment of human destiny, except the Divine law, the *Torah* of Moses. In Islam it is the *Shari'a* that guarantees man's twofold happiness, in this world and in the next. Maimonides speaks, as we know, of the twofold perfection of body and faith. He draws a distinction between the *Torah* as the only guarantor of both by fulfilling the *mitsvot*, the ceremonial and the judicial laws. His intellectualism made him stress intellectual perfection as the highest perfection on the basis of ethical perfection, in the wake of Aristotle. The perception of God is possible only through the possession of the intellectual virtues to perfection, and this is possible for the philosopher alone; another example of Greek influence. It is tempered with the Jewish view that God's essence cannot be understood, only His actions. But perception is crowned by the love of God which Maimonides defines as "imitation of God". This term is Plato's for whom *homoiosis theou* means "to become just, holy and wise". It matters little whether this concept has come to Al-Fārābī— Maimonides's probable source—from Plato's *Theaetetus* or, more likely, from Plotinus's *Enneads*. What does matter is how Maimonides understood it in the context of Judaism. As we would expect, Maimonides illustrates it with a quotation from *Sifrē* to Deuteronomy 10. 12, an interpretation of Leviticus 19. 2: "As He is gracious, so be thou gracious; as He is merciful so be thou merciful". What he means is that man must imitate God's ways, that is His thirteen attributes; and he demands of the prophetic lawgiver and leader precisely this: he must imitate God because "His actions (the thirteen attributes are—since God has no qualities—attributes of action, all of them those of mercy with the exception of Exodous 34. 4) are necessary for the government of States." The political importance is clear; it goes back to Plato.

Now, we have seen that justice is the most important political virtue. Hence, Plato and his Muslim and Jewish disciples probably mean the same. Wisdom, whether philosophical or *Torah*-wisdom, provides sufficient common ground between the two cultures and can easily be adapted to Muslim and Jewish monotheism. But when we come to "holiness" it is clear that the God of Israel is not the God of Plato. Hence, a considerable modification is called for. The *Torah* is, however, quite explicit on this point: "Ye shall be holy: for I the Lord your God am holy" (Leviticus 19. 2) and many other passages, such as Deuteronomy 7. 6; 14.2, 21, etc. That Maimonides understood it in this sense can hardly be doubted in view of his exposition quoted above. While we must be careful not to take a passage out of its context, isolate it and then use it to prove a theory, it is right to say that taking the *Guide* and the Code as a whole and realising the almost identical treatment of the *mitsvot* in the third book of the *Guide* and in the Code, Maimonides stood four square on the ground of Judaism in his acceptance and adaptation of Greek philosophy to his exposition of Judaism for the intellectual élite of his generation. He expressly contrasted the *Torah* with human laws "like the laws of the Greeks ..." This means that he did not accept Plato's state as the ideal polity, another reason for rejecting the equation of the prophetic lawgiver with the philosopher-king.

Maimonides was strongly influenced by Al-Fārābī and his presentation of Platonic politics. It helped him to see the political significance of the *Torah* much more clearly. But of at least equal significance is his departure from his source.

All medieval religious thinkers are preoccupied with the idea of happiness which the individual can achieve only as a citizen of the State. For the Muslim it is the *Sharī ‘a*-State and for the Jew the *Torah*-State which enables man to reach his goal.

Aristotle distinguishes the ultimate, highest happiness from less perfect kinds of happiness, such as honour, riches, or pleasure. But for him these inferior kinds may also constitute true happiness for those who strive for them. Al-Fārābī calls these 'lower' forms imaginary happiness and distinguishes them from true happiness which is attainable only in the ideal State (of Plato and of Islam). The other kinds of happiness belong to Plato's imperfect states. Maimonides accepts this distinction—he uses the same Arabic term for imaginary happiness—but, unlike Al-Fārābī, he reserves true happiness to the *Torah*-State and denies it to Plato's ideal state in which the citizens can reach only imaginary happiness, since the *Nomos*, so he maintains, provides only for the welfare of the body. That he disregarded Plato's ultimate aim is characteristic of his exclusive recognition of the *Torah* as leading to God. He completely overlooked the fact that right beliefs and sound opinions are demanded as indispensible by Plato just as much as they are by the *Torah*, as Jewish philosophers point out.

The extension of true happiness to the world-to-come is a further example of that blending of Greek, Jewish and Muslim ideas which is so characteristic of medieval thinkers. Ultimate perfection and happiness can be attained only in the world to come. This rabbinic doctrine is acepted by all so-called philosophers from Sa'adya to Albo. The same applies to Islam and its *Sharī‘a*. The identity of aim between religion and philosophy is actually deduced from the concept of happiness, irrespective of the fact that it is originally alien to both religions. That it is given a decisive turn towards the religious domain is seen not only in the equation of happiness with the "imitation of God", but also in the conviction that happiness in its full significance will come to the believer who combines intellectual perfection with loving service of God, in the hereafter. Perception, fear and love of God together constitute that service of God which leads us to our destiny and destination.

Sa'adya had already spoken of man's duty to let reason prevail over nature as the ineluctable condition for the attainment of happiness. It is the aim of the *Torah* "to make the servants of God entirely happy". Philo had already declared that happiness is the result of the complete fulfilment of the *Torah*.

Despite all the emphasis on the intellectual duty of knowledge of God, all Jewish medieval thinkers point to the *Torah* as the guide to ethics. Social justice is a necessary condition for the attainment of happiness. For Sa'adya, the creation of the world is designed by God to ensure the happiness of man who serves Him in gratitude in a moral life. God created man out of love and mercy. Why did God not grant man happiness without the commandments and prohibitions of the *Torah*? Sa'adya answers that eternal bliss was preferable as the result of the fulfilment of the *Torah* since reason argues that he who works for the highest good receives a double share as compared with him who attains bliss by Divine grace alone.

ETHICAL VIRTUES

Abraham ibn Da'ud devotes the third part of his *Exalted Faith* to Practical Philosophy, but, unlike Avicenna, treats of prophecy in the second part as one of the fundamental doctrines of the faith because it is closely linked with the revelation of the *Torah* in history. Thus, he concentrates in this part, entitled—after Plato—*On the cure of the soul*, on ethics and the several commandments. Happiness or bliss depends on the improvement of morals, which in turn depends on the political and religious laws in force in the State. His indebtedness to Plato's fourth book of the *Republic* cannot be discussed here. We can only mention that justice has first place in his scheme, closely following Plato. But Abraham ibn Da'ud adds to the social virtue the individual-religious one, for justice and righteousness also form the first religious duty: they must govern man's relations with God as well as with his fellow men.

We know that cultic duties are for the Greeks political duties. In Judaism, as we learn from Abraham ibn Da'ud man who cannot show gratitude to God for benefactions received through Divine mercy by righteous deeds, must at least thank God through prayer in worship. He thus looks upon prayer both as an individual-religious and a social duty. Cult and ritual alone are not sufficient to attain happiness, man must also serve God in all he does all the time. Moses is for Abraham ibn Da'ud the exemplar of righteousness: God called him to His service on account of his ethical perfection. God made Moses promulgate the *Torah* to improve the world and bring mankind near to God. In Moses, justice and righteousness are joined by humility. Abraham ibn Da'ud adds religious virtues to the social ones in order to give practical philosophy a religious foundation and direction.

Significantly, for him the Ten Commandments are the result of Divine providence and care. The first five are concerned with man's duties to God and the second half with interhuman relations. They are on the religious plane what practical philosophy assigns to economics and ethics. The only difference is that as they come from God they are absolutely perfect. Similarly, political laws guarantee the good order of the world. Society depends on them for its continued existence. The *Torah* ensures this to perfection. The first social command is love of one's neighbour; then follow honesty in business dealings, just measure and weight, prohibition of interest and usury, care of the poor and the stranger, remission of debts, redemption of slaves and other laws enjoined in the *Torah*, which is thus proved to be the best social legislation. Love of one's neighbour is a social-religious commandment, and the law of sacrifices, a revealed law, the usefulness of which is unknown to us, completes the regulations of the divine law.

That Abraham ibn Da'ud includes purely religious laws like sacrifices, ritual (phylacteries, etc.) and other ceremonial laws is intentional. He wants to show that the *Torah* comprises not only the whole range of theoretical and practical philosophy, but in addition something which human law lacks because it does not stem from God, the God of justice, righteousness and love. Hence his division of the laws of the *Torah* into doctrines, that is beliefs and convictions, as the most important theoretical commandments. They are followed by the ethical commandments, then by laws governing the family (economics), next by political laws and finally by laws designed by Divine wisdom. The first and last groups place the *Torah* above philosophy and make it thus the best guide to happiness. By making beliefs and convictions into religious duties he wants to give them the status of absolute values coming from divine wisdom, just as with the ceremonial laws. But even so, he requires theoretical philosophy to guide man to their understanding!

That there is not always consistency in this division and in making an overall claim for religion to what can also be assigned to philosophy, only shows how the boundary between faith and reason sometimes becomes blurred in the attempt to reconcile both realms with each other. But the extension of the range of the *Torah*, due to its Divine nature and the addition to the four cardinal virtues of Plato of such purely religious virtues as love of neighbour, humility, piety and devotion, are clearly intended to vindicate the superiority of the *Torah* over the *Nomos* as the true guide to true happiness and eternal bliss.

Herein all religious thinkers are at one, the adherents of philosophy as well as its opponents. Jewish life must be guided by the *Torah*.

AFFINITIES WITH SUFISM

It remains to refer briefly to a remarkable work of Jewish theology which bears some resemblance to similar writings originating in Sufism or Muslim mysticism. Bachya ibn Pakuda's *Guide to the Duties of the Heart* is an ethical treatise with a strong intellectual flavour. The very title points to Sufism. His aim is to call attention to the greater importance of the duties of the heart than of the duties of the members, that is, external duties, on the basis of the knowledge of God. The book is in form and arrangement close to Sufi ethical treatises. It illustrates the author's thesis at all stages with stories and metaphors taken from the Bible and rabbinic literature and also from Sufi literature but in such a way that the uninitiated would never suspect their foreign origin. For Bachya has so completely succeeded in imbuing his material with deep Jewish religiosity and Jewish religious concepts.

Philosophically Bachya is near to Neo-platonism in its Islamic form; traces of *Kalam* are also to be found. But he does not reach the independent creativeness of the first Neo-platonic Jewish philosopher in Spain, Ibn Gabirol, whose *Source of Life* had such an influence on the scholastics who never suspected that its author was a Jew. What appealed to generations of Jews from Bachya's own day right down to ours is his skilful combination of these elements with indigenous biblical and rabbinic concepts and tales. He appeals to religious feeling and pious devotion and stresses the ethical obligations of man. The book consists of ten "gates" which represent so many stages on the journey of the religious seeker to God, not the God of the mystics, but the God of the Bible. Bachya was an ascetic, not a mystic. At the beginning of the upward journey there stands the affirmation of the absolute oneness and unity of God. This is the necessary foundation, the first "gate". To affirm and assert the absolute unity of God is man's first and foremost duty. The duties of the heart are postulated by Revelation and by Reason. "God has opened three gates to the understanding of His religion and His *Torah*: 1. a sound intellect; 2. the true Book of God, revealed to the prophet (Moses); and 3. the traditions received from our ancestors, who received them from the prophets."

We are familiar with this definition of religious knowledge from Sa'adya. It is important to realise the intellectual basis of the inner duties which, together with the external duties must be carefully rendered to God. Reason has been implanted in man that he may the better obtain certainty about both Revelation and Tradition, so that his faith and conduct may be based on Reason and Tradition. But it is equally important to note that Reason is in the service of Revelation so that its meaning may be grasped better and man thus be better equipped for serving God in love. Conversely, the *Torah* comes to the aid of Reason, the *Torah* which comes from a benevolent God whose many benefactions we enjoy. We must show our love in gratitude through actions pleasing to God. The *Torah* tells us what these actions are; it teaches us the way to God by the fear of punishment for transgression and the hope of reward in this and in the next world for obedience to the Divine Will. Bachya emphasises that to please God is the real reason for the fulfilment of the commandments and is more meritorious than the reward we will receive. Our intellect proceeds from this stage ever higher to a fuller understanding of God. The greater our knowledge of God becomes, the better we are able to free our souls from the prison of our senses.

This Platonic idea of the soul imprisoned in the body and striving through purification to free itself and to return to its heavenly abode is met with in medieval Jewish philosophy several times. But whereas it is autonomous reason with Plato which achieves this desirable end, for Bachya (and others) it is reason bound by fear, knowledge and love of God. It is for this reason that his ethical treatise begins with a philsophical disquisition about the unity of God. Bachya is aware of the fact that intellectually men are different from each other and that not every one can gain a knowledge of God by intellectual striving. He refuses to separate the few elect from the masses and to make the attainment of human happiness dependent on intellectual perfection. The naive, sincerely pious and devout Jew is not debarred from loving God and being loved by Him as long as he wholeheartedly fulfils the *mitsvot*, both the external and inner duties, but especially the latter. In faith and devotion we can all be equals, and we can all obtain our share of happiness. Bachya, who gave humility a place of honour among the duties of the heart, spurned intellectual conceit. The riches of the inner life, at peace with God and with His creation, are within the reach of all who seek God in fear and love. "Love thy neighbour as thyself" permeates every sincere believer's life with a radiance and an ability to experience and practise the "joy of the commandment" whatever his intellectual attainment may be.

And yet, Bachya could say that the faith of the believer is not complete unless he *knows* and fulfils the duties of the heart. What he means by knowledge is indicated in his statement, based on Psalm 51: "behold, thou desirest truth in the inward parts; make me therefore to know wisdom in mine innermost heart". It is contained in and acquired by the science which he, in Sufi-fashion, characterises as "the light of the hearts and the brilliance of the souls". We have here an illuminating example of a Sufi interpretation of a biblical passage and at the same time a scriptural confirmation of a Sufi idea. But it would be wrong to dismiss rational knowledge as being transformed into inner awareness, as one might be tempted to do by this example. For Bachya insists that he who is gifted with sound intellect has the inescapable duty of verifying the teachings of the Bible—with the help of reason and tradition, supporting this demand with Isaiah 40, 48. He appeals to rabbinic tradition in Mishna and Talmud to show that our sages were more intent on the performance of the inner duties than on legal rules. Naturally he accepts the obligation of all commandments as laid down by the rabbis. But he finds solid support for the duties of the heart in the *Torah*, for "the actions demanded by God are firmly rooted in sincerity of hearts and purity of innermost thoughts".

The roots of these duties are ten, hence he arranges his book in ten "gates". We must render God invisible as well as visible service. Prayer, fasting, and charity are the outward manifestations, the inward service consists in our thoughts. The first gate has already been discussed; the second demands a positive attitude to our fellow men. This is important because it mellows Bachya's asceticism which is free from gloom and despondency. "Acceptance of the service of God" is next, followed by "Trust (and confidence) in God"; "Dedication of all our acts to God"; "Humility in face of His unique Sovereignty"; "Repentance"; "Self-examination"; "Asceticism"; and finally "The love of God". In this the pilgrimage to God culminates.

In fact, the whole book is in a sense an extended commentary on the two verses in Deuteronomy 6. 4-5: the *Shema'* and the command to love God. Space does not permit us to quote from Bachya at length, but a few characteristic phrases must be adduced by way of illustration to show how he adapted Sufi concepts and their realisation in Islam in a rigorously ascetic mysticism to the social ethics of Judaism. The interesting point is that Bachya used Sufi terms but gave them a meaning consonant with Jewish concepts.

By "self-examination" he means taking counsel with oneself in relation to the demands of God and how to serve Him. Of trust in God he says: "The man who directs his soul towards God, with him the Creator will be. He will relieve him of his depression, will quieten his heart from its fear, open to him the gates leading to the knowledge of God, reveal to him the mysteries of His wisdom ... He will see without eyes, hear without ears, speak without a tongue, feel things without the relevant senses and apprehend them without reasoning. He will not be impatient with any situation in his circumstances nor prefer any other lot than that which God has chosen for him" (Hyamson). This is the nearest approach to mysticism in Bachya. But it does not mean the same thing as the Arabic term of which *bitachon* is the Hebrew translation. For trust and devotion is not self-abandonment in mystical union with the Divine, complete self-abnegation, just as asceticism for Bachya is not the complete negation of the world, of the senses. For God has created man out of love and wants mankind to endure.

Bachya only stresses the transience of our mundane life: "Wilt thou not awake, my brother, and realise how you have striven for something imperfect and have hurried to attain it in order to keep your body in normal condition, though it will be associated with you only for a short while ... (when) it should be our duty to be ready for the appointed time and prepare ourselves for the distant journey to the other world ... The road is long, the resting place far off. Why have we not taken it to heart to remember our latter end? ... We have occupied ourselves with a world that passes, and left out of consideration the world that endures. We have concerned ourselves with our physical ailments and have forgotten our spiritual maladies. We have engaged in the service of our evil inclination, and have abandoned the service of Him who created us" (Hyamson). This is clearly the mood of an ascetic.

But although Bachya recommends the renunciation of the pleasures of the world for their own sake he would allow radical severance of social ties only to a few exceptional persons. He says: "Solitude and seclusion from people save us from all the sins we have mentioned (adultery, fraud, perjury, false testimony, etc.) and are the most powerful means for securing good qualities. But be also careful not to be misled by the fancy that association with wise men who know God and His law and mingling with great men deprive one of the advantages of solitude and cause the value of isolation to disappear. That only applies to complete solitude and total isolation. But association with men of generous and kindly disposition and with those who study the *Torah*, has important advantages. These excel the merits of solitude ..." (Hyamson).

Bachya explicitly states that, according to the *Torah*, the proper kind of asceticism is not seclusion and separation, but friendliness towards our fellow men and the performance within society of all the duties of the heart. We should isolate the soul which is a stranger in this world, and turn it to the love of the Creator. To this last gate—the love of God—

everything else is only preparatory. Fear of God precedes the love of God. Asceticism is no less essential since we cannot love God with our heart if the love of the world has taken root in it. We should aim at complete concentration on God in trust and love, in our thoughts and in our actions. It is thus clear that love of God does not end in mystical union with God, but in the willing obedience to His will, in fear and reverence and in joyful performance of the ethical duties He has imposed on us, in society. The discipline of the *Torah* has prevented him from eschewing social responsibility, from extreme other-worldliness, and has made him counsel moderation and inwardness.

In one point, his Muslim environment seems to have gained ascendancy over a principal tenet of his Judaism: he wavers between Islamic predestination and Jewish freewill. Man has the choice of obeying or disobeying the divine Will; but once he has made the choice, the course of his actions is set. This is, however, clearly contradicted by his stress on repentance and atonement.

His guide to inwardness and personal and social ethics, written in Arabic in Spain—he was a *dayan* (judge)—in Saragossa or Cordova towards the end of the eleventh century, was translated into Hebrew in the last third of the twelfth century and has exerted a tremendous influence on countless generations. It has also stimulated a whole literary genre, our *Mussar*-literature, from Abraham Maimuni through the eighteenth-century Moses Chayim Luzzatto to the ethical literature of Chassidism.

Maimuni's *Comprehensive Guide for the Servants of God*, or, as the part which is translated into English is called by Rosenblatt, its editor, *The Highways to Perfection* is of the same type; it has a philosophical basis and commends study and contemplation in order to perfect the soul engaged in the service of God in sincerity and humility. The Highest

I

Good consists in the "clinging to God" (*devekut*). The Sufi influence is more apparent in Maimuni's language than in that of Bachya. *The Highways* lead to perfection which, in its highest degree, vouchsafed to very few, reaches ecstasy in the soul when the body and its members are made to praise God in love. The divine light shines upon the soul in the state of *devekut*. Perfection implies perfect fulfilment of the *Torah* and is but the prelude to perfection in the world-to-come. The esoteric, inner, mystical sense of the *Torah* is accessible to few pure, humble and sincere souls only.

Sufi traits are clearly discernible even more in Maimuni than in Bachya. They are blended with Jewish traditional thought and conduct which they help to bring into focus. Men like these and their books perform a vital function in Judaism, in that they remind us of the duties of the heart and call upon us to restore the balance between them and the duties of the members.

JUDAISM ASSERTS ITSELF

Affinity and contrast between Islam and Judaism have given rise, as is only natural, to controversy. We said something about this when we surveyed the Jewish element in Islam. Jewish literature in Arabic and in Hebrew is full of polemical and apologetic references which reflect Muslim attacks, objections and charges. We have heard of the charge that the Jews had falsified their Scriptures and we have reviewed the work of Bible commentators, Halachists and religious philosophers, devoted without exception to strengthening Judaism in the minds of successive generations of Jews living in Islamic surroundings and subjected to doubt and confusion from without and within.

Yehuda Halevi's *Kuzari* contains anti-Islamic polemics as

does Maimonides's *Guide*. We know that Sa'adya Gaon refuted rationalist critique of the Bible and heretical and sectarian attacks on rabbanite Judaism, principally launched by the Karaites. Jewish converts to Islam wrote against Judaism in self-defence of their defection and out of conversionist zeal in the hope of winning their former coreligionists over to the new faith. This naturally provoked counter-attack in defence of Judaism. It has been shown that Karaite authors refer the "little horn" of Daniel, Chapter 7, to the reign of Ishmael (Islam). Religious poetry abounds with polemical allusions to Ishmael, "the son of the maidservant". The Jews had to refute the Muslim claim that Mohammed's abrogation of one law justified the abrogation of the whole law, i.e. that the *Torah* had been superseded.

We saw earlier that Maimonides distinguished between the prophet sent by God with a law and the other prophets who foretell the future and warn a sinful nation. Abraham ibn Ezra in his Commentary on Genesis makes the same distinction between a "messenger" and "prophets (foretelling) the future". Altogether, commentaries are frequently used for polemics. This was an important means of strengthening Jewish faith in Judaism and in Messianic redemption. This applies to anti-Muslim as well as to anti-Christian polemics: such statements were not primarily intended to convince the opponent, but to fortify and arm one's own side.

Of special interest in this connection is a treatise written in Hebrew by a pupil of Nachamanides, Rabbi Solomon ben Adret of Barcelona, the noted Halachist and literary opponent of the Dominican Raimundus Martini. Although living in Christian Spain, our Rabbi felt called upon to reply to an attack by the eleventh century Muslim theologian, controversialist and poet Ibn Ḥazm. Ibn Ḥazm's *Book of Religions and Sects*, one of the earliest contributions to the

comparative history of religion, attacked the very basis of
Judaism, the *Torah*, as something which only a few indi-
viduals, namely the priests, possessed. He said that it had
been tampered with during the Hebrew monarchy, and only
Ezra had reinstated and made it known to the people. This
and other accusations were refuted by Solomon b. Adret
with the usual arguments, the chief among them being that
the authority of the *Torah*, its revelation from Sinai, was
witnessed not only by one prophet but also by six hundred
thousand Israelites assembled at the foot of Sinai.

Another distinguished rabbi, Simon b. Zemach Duran
(1361-1444), who had spent most of his life in Muslim surroundings in Algiers, devoted a part of a long religio-
philosophical introduction to his commentary on *Pirke Avot*
to a polemical defence of the *Torah* against Christianity and
Islam.

It is only fair to say that under Islam Judaism and its adherents had not to endure anything like the sustained,
officially sponsored and relentlessly conducted attack of the
Christian Church on Jews in Christian lands. There was not
that same concerted attempt at wholesale conversion—with
the notable exception of Almohad fanaticism in Spain when
Jews and Christians were faced with the inescapable choice
of conversion to the dominant faith of Islam or death. In
these circumstances, anti-Muslim polemics were out of the
question. If we compare Maimonides's lenient attitude
to forced conversion as with his pupil Joseph ibn Aknin's
severe strictures we must make due allowance for the
time lag. When Maimonides wrote his *Letter on Conversion*
this step did not entail more than the pronouncement
by the convert of the formula of the unity of God and the
apostleship of Mohammed. But later the Almohades became more rigid and demanding and were no longer satisfied with mere lip-service. Maimonides and Ibn Aknin

counselled emigration to less fanatical Muslim lands and it is highly probable that the departure of the Maimonides family from Cordova to Fez is closely connected with such a move. Josef ibn Aknin wrote in 1191, full of self-accusation for his temporary defection, and suggested immediate exile to escape from the intolerable dilemma. That Maimonides's strictures of Mohammed in his *Guide* could be written is due to his being domiciled in Egypt at the time of writing his principal philosophical work in 1190.

By and large, anti-Jewish attack was directed against individual prominent Jews who had risen to positions of great influence and wealth in the service of Muslim princes.

POETRY

Controversy and occasional persecution are inevitable elements of Jewish existence in the *Galut* even under such favourable conditions as obtained under Islam. Yet, to repeat, there is no period in the history of Jewish dispersion comparable to that under Muslim rule in the Middle Ages, which permitted such a flowering of the Hebraic genius, such a fruitful meeting of Judaism with other cultures which resulted in such a rich and varied literature. Re-interpretation led to consolidation, the challenge of Islamic culture and civilisation to a vivid awakening of the national-religious consciousness which expressed itself in the systematic study of the bases of Jewish creed and law and led to a new appreciation of the Holy Tongue and its excellence.

This can nowhere be seen and experienced more clearly and forcefully than in the abundant harvest of Hebrew poetry, both sacred and secular. Liturgical poetry flourished from the sixth century onwards, and its significance for the religious life of countless generations of Jews can hardly be overestimated. Its richest flowering, however, falls in the "Golden Age of Spain", though the share of Babylonia should not be forgotten. That indefatigable pioneer of a vigorous literary renaissance of Judaism, Sa'adya Gaon, added many a *piyut* to those known in his time, as his recently edited *Siddur* shows. Thus, he contributed to our liturgy no less than to the other branches of our literature. We all know how faithfully our liturgy reflects not only the prayers, but also the hopes and disappointments of generations of loyal Jews, largely from the poetical additions to our daily and festival prayers which afford us this welcome glimpse into the hearts and minds of past generations.

One of the glories of modern Jewish learning is that it has opened our eyes by giving us the first systematic collection and description of medieval religious poetry. L. Zunz mapped out the field and assembled and evaluated enough material to enable his successors to build an imposing edifice on his foundations. The Cairo *Geniza* has not yet been exhausted and distinguished present-day scholars are adding constantly to this unique treasure by their skill and patient labour. It is not possible to do justice to both sacred and secular poetry of the period under discussion in this sketch. The reader is referred to a well-balanced, authoritative survey by one of the foremost workers in this field, Professor Shalom Spiegel, in Vol. II of *The Jews*, under the title *On Medieval Hebrew Poetry* and to S. W. Baron's *A Social and Religious History of the Jews*, Vol. VII, on both of which I have drawn.

A few general remarks are, however, necessary. That sacred poetry should be cultivated by Jews living in a religious civilisation is not surprising. The excellent custom of enlivening the fixed ritual of daily, Sabbath and festival prayers by appropriate additions grew in volume from the days of Yannai (*c.* 550 C.E.) onwards. Not only have many pieces been added; their artistry and religious depth and emotion have been developed to a remarkable degree so that they stand out not only as literary creations but also as monuments to the unshakable faith of Jews in God and His protection of Israel in adversity and in the fulfilment of His promise of redemption and restoration. These compositions saved prayer from becoming a routine, a mere duty; they helped to retain and increase the spontaneous character of worship on the individual and social-communal levels; they poured new life and significance into the ancient prayers of the Synagogue. Inasmuch as the liturgy reflects the life and thought of the worshippers bringing before God praise and thanks for His bounty and protection, imprecation for His help in trouble and in danger, joy and sorrow, hope and despair, much can be learnt about Jewish history from the *Siddur* in its many rites and above all about steadfastness to Jewish ideals and loyalty to tradition.

Ibn Gabirol wrote much religious poetry of a strongly individual expression of faith and loyalty in adversity. The power of prayer, purifying and uplifting, comforting and reassuring, speaks to us in many poems, one of which *Royal Crown* is read on the Day of Atonement in many congregations. Shemuel haNagid, vizier of Granada, talmudist, patron and controversialist who was flourishing when Ibn Ḥazm wrote in Cordova, is also renowned as a religious, and even more as a secular, poet. Yehuda Halevi is unsurpassed as a singer of God and Zion, of friendship and love. Moses ibn Ezra wrote not only superb poems, but also a most learned treatise on the art of poetry.

Instead of adducing a string of illustrious names of highly-gifted poets let us pause for a moment and remember the revolution that came over Hebrew poetry, which had hitherto been confined to adding sacred lyrics to the poetry of the Bible. No literary activity so closely reflects the high

degree of assimilation to the Muslim way of life as does the
secular poetry of the Spanish Jews. Those just mentioned are
only a few of the most successful who produced sacred as
well as mundane lyrics. It goes without saying that even in
their religious songs they employed Arabic metres which
they heard at the courts and in the streets of Moorish Spain.
The flexibility of the Holy Tongue was immeasurably enhanced under their skilful hands. In their secular songs in
praise of princes and patrons, in "taunt songs" with dam-
aging effect, full of scorn and contempt, dismay and anger,
in singing of love, courtly and less courtly, of the beauty and
womanly charms of the beloved, even of the beauty of boys,
they imitated the themes and forms of Arab poetry. In the
view of experts, they could hold their own against the best
of the Arab poets who were their teachers. What is so
amazing is the frequent, sudden bursting of the local con-
vention by a deliberate application of a mundane atmosphere
to the religious concepts of Judaism in the most sublime
transformation.

The inherited treasure of religious and ethical thought
and feeling breaks through the sophisticated, not to say
decadent, moral and social conventions of high society
which gave rise to their poems. When we read these poems
from the eleventh to the fourteenth century we can sense
the power and the glory of Muslim rule at its height and
at its best: but we also witness the decline that set in when
Christianity began to reconquer Spain and to oust Muslim
power, though not so easily its culture and civilisation.

The Hebrew poetry of the period is also instructive in
another respect: the brilliance and skill of making verses
(which could often mean one thing and its direct opposite,
praise or blame; it depended how you read it), the virtuosity
of a courtier's flattery and wit, could not stifle for long the
feeling of insecurity and the questioning as to how long the

grand life would last. Yehuda Halevi stands out as the singer of Zion, of homesickness for the land of the fathers amidst the scintillating splendour of Ishmael. He longs for *Erets Yisrael*, for divine redemption, and he forsakes the glitter for his vision: he embarks on the journey to the Holy Land. Has he realised his noble dream? We only know that he died on his way to Zion: it would be comforting to think that he reached his destination. "My heart is in the East, and I in the far West, How can I savour food, and find in it delight? How shall I pay my vows and self-denying oaths, When Zion bows to Edom, and I to Arab might? I find it easy to leave all the bounty of Spain, And to cherish instead the dust on the Temple's site"(Baron's rendering). How many Jews has this impassioned song inspired down to our own day!

A VIEW OF JEWISH HISTORY

This longing for redemption and restoration naturally leads us to ask finally: what did leading minds in this most colourful age so rich in material and spiritual achievement think of the meaning and purpose of Jewish history? First of all, why should there be this Messianic hope and expectation in a Jewish society which was less segregated and consequently much more integrated in the general (Muslim) society than any Jewry of the time, or before or for long after? The assimilation mentioned earlier on cannot have been so close and effective if just in Spain—where Judaism was confronted with Islam and Christianity locked in battle—three thinkers attempted an answer to the millenial question: what is the meaning and purpose of Jewish suffering? For Spanish Jewry had this searching question thrust upon it from the eleventh century onwards just as

German and French Jewry did during the Crusades. The difference is that wholesale persecution and massacre hit Spanish Jewry much later and that the more spacious and prosperous life in Muslim society made leading Spanish Jews extend the question from Jewish suffering to the meaning of Jewish and world history.

Their theology of history was formulated successively by Abraham bar Chiya, Yehuda Halevi and Don Isaac Abravanel. Since the last mentioned lived in Christian Spain until the expulsion in 1492, we will confine our brief summary to Yehuda Halevi and to his contemporary Abraham bar Chiya of Barcelona in the early twelfth century. This great astronomer and mathematician was also an important theological polemicist of great force and conviction. Since Spain was the meeting place of Christianity and Islam, with both in their most militant frame of mind, much of our author's argument and exposition reflects that conflict in its bearing on the Jews which Yehuda Halevi so aptly summarised when he said that "Christian and Muslim share the whole world between them" and "they wage their wars and drag us down in their fall". These words form the background against which the thinking of their generation about the Jewish fate proceeded.

In his defence of Judaism, Abraham bar Chiya turned much of Christian theory and anti-Jewish argument and also Muslim theological attack polemically against both. He combined Rabbinic tradition with Neo-platonic philosophy as known to him from Arabic sources and astrology into a Jewish answer to the Christian view expressed by St. Augustine, which was then the regnant theory of history. He accepted in part the Christian doctrine of original sin and the Muslim theory of prophecy, but bent both, in an attenuated form, into the service of his Jewish answer. His theory cannot be reported in full. Only his application of the Islamic doctrine of prophetic illumination or light in a characteristically Jewish form can be briefly stated.

This special gift was first bestowed by God on Adam. After his fall the light was inherited by the most worthy individual in every following generation down to Noah and Abraham. Islam claims that from Abraham, the first Muslim, as we remember, it was received by Mohammed, "the seal of the prophets". Abraham bar Chiya denies it to Mohammed altogether and instead lets it descend from Abraham to Isaac, from him to Jacob and his twelve sons. He extends it in this way to their descendants, the twelve tribes, by linking it with the Jewish idea of the election of Israel and transforms the individual "prophetic light" into the inalienable possession of the people of Israel who stood at the foot of Mount Sinai. He thus identifies the concept of the "prophetic light" with that of the covenant. God binds Israel to Himself through the covenant they made voluntarily with Him, just as He had previously bound the patriarchs to Himself by an individual covenant made between Him and Abraham, Isaac and Jacob. From now on, Abraham bar Chiya follows the pattern of biblical history (redemption from Egypt, election, rebellion, repentance, Messianic redemption) and lays particular stress on repentance here and now in order to bring about the promised redemption "speedily and in our days". The biological concept of inherited election was developed by Yehuda Halevi.

Before we speak of him, a few words about Abraham bar Chiya's attempt at calculating the end-time. He does this on the three-fold basis of biblical prophecy in Daniel, rabbinic world periods of three times two thousand years, and planetary constellations. Sa'adya Gaon had already computed the advent of the Messiah on the basis of Daniel 7, 25. So did Abraham bar Chiya and after him Abravanel, each

arriving at a different date, naturally! Messianic belief and
expectation have always been strong among Jews. In our
case, our distinguished astronomer had recourse to this
science (of which astrology in those days was a legitimate
branch) in order to fan the embers of hope in his generation.
Faith in the divine plan unfolding in history and exemplified
in the history of His chosen people —the exclusive, hereditary possessor of the Light—inspired him to read the stars in
order to determine when the meaning of history was to be
fulfilled in the Messianic restoration of the Jewish people to
its homeland.

Yehuda Halevi was as averse to Messianic speculation,
frowned upon by tradition, as to the use of astrology in its
service. It was incompatible with his fervent belief and
confident trust in the divine promise of redemption.

But in his *Kuzari* he makes much of the same idea as that
expressed in the "prophetic light" of Abraham bar Chiya,
whether he knew it or not: he calls it "the divine thing" or
"matter". It sets Israel apart from the other nations as God's
"peculiar treasure" or "kingdom of priests". Needless to
say, Adam's fall has for him no influence at all on the
ultimate redemption of Israel.

It is true that for Abraham bar Chiya it is the *Torah* from
Sinai, and not the death of Jesus, which achieves the gradual
recession of man's lower nature and promotes the rule of the
rational part of the soul through repentance and atonement.
But he would not let the Christians and Muslims, at whose
hands the Jewish people suffered so much, share in resurrection and redemption. 'Nationalistic' as Yehuda Halevi's
reservation of the "divine thing" to Israel may be, his concept of redemption is all-embracing, since in the Messianic
era the Gentiles too will be redeemed, as the prophets foretell their acceptance of the One and Only God. The moral
laws are given to all mankind. Yet the prophetic spirit is

exclusive to Israel, according to Halevi, because it is a bio-
logically hereditary force or principle. Why modern Jews
should be shocked at this "narrow nationalism" is difficult
to understand if we look at Yehuda Halevi's age and its
particular circumstances. God's providence watches over
all nations, but indirectly, through the planets under whose
rule they live. Only Israel is under direct divine rule, without
intermediary planets. This is also the view of Don Isaac
Abravanel at the end of the fifteenth century and underlies
his Messianic treatises.

Medieval Jewry resembles earlier generations in sharing
with them the unresolved tension between the universal and
particularist aspects of Judaism. The unity of God demands
the unity of mankind; yet Israel is to be "a holy nation" and
"a kingdom of priests". The peculiar position of Israel is
emphasised by Yehuda Halevi in his insistence on the in-
dissoluble unity of People, *Torah* and Land of Israel. In his
view, the climate of *Erets Yisrael* is particularly suited to a
life of sincere faith and religious devotion which must be
sustained by wholehearted fulfilment of the *mitsvot* of the
divine *Torah*. The more deeply is he distressed to see a large
number of his generation put up with the inferior status of
Galut, with such ease and self-satisfaction. *Galut* is punishment for our sins; it teaches us humility and demands of us
repentance and atonement by making us long for the return
to Zion in a spirit of meekness and loyalty to our religious
institutions and our ancestors. There, in *Erests Yisrael*, lies
our salvation, and not in suffering scattered among the
nations. We may call his view of the special character of
Israel chauvinistic and may think that it ill accords with their
admittedly insecure but much higher social position and
cultural level under Islam. But this would be a shortsighted
view since it is precisely this outwardly most favoured posi-
in the *Galut* which underlined for Yehuda Halevi the

unnaturalness and, in the final analysis, the precarious danger of Israel in the *Galut*. What is still more important is the fact, amply borne out by his *Kuzari* and by his religious poetry, that he had a clear vision of the ideal Israel, in contrast to Christian and Muslim claims to be, in a Christian phrase, "the true Israel".

We must realise that, narrow and naturalistic as his religious nationalism was, it was so for two very good reasons. In the first place, biblical and rabbinic teaching about the special relationship between God and Israel symbolised by the Covenant had an inner reality for Halevi which not only made him see more clearly the tragedy of Jewish life in the *Galut*—which roused him to a "defence of the despised religion"—but also helped him to view the *Galut* with the eyes of one who was filled with faith in Israel, the loyal partner of the Covenant from Sinai. Secondly, in his journey to Palestine, the land of Israel, he conquered personal honour and admiration and national prestige and position as a member of the most civilised part of the congregation of Israel. By his own example he wanted to show the way to salvation which only he who accepts for himself and his people the pattern of history which begins with the redemption from Egyptian bondage and ends with the redemption of the return to Zion can truly seek and desire. True to the biblical promise, he prayed and hoped for salvation *of* the Jews, but also of mankind *through* the Jews. Maimonides is in basic agreement with such a view; for him, Messianism is the meaning of Jewish history and restoration its consummation.

Thus, Halevi ceases to be a medieval Jew interesting to read and apt to make us feel proud or ashamed, as the case may be. He throws out a challenge to us no less than to his own generation—a challenge not only of faith, but also of action based on such faith. What do we mean by *Galut*? Today, Yehuda Halevi's works are not just so many pages of a glorious literature of the past which we read, put aside as antiquated and forgotten in the material comforts of a meanlingless twentieth century. We must make a decision in the light of his challenge. For, let us make no mistake about it: he may be wrong in his exclusiveness, but he is right in the premise which led him to it: the call of "the divine thing", the message of the prophets to a torn, strife-ridden world to return to the moral laws of the *Torah* which we Jews, above all other people, have an obligation to implement, because they were given to us once with the obligation of the Covenant and because we owe our survival to them.

WHAT OF THE FUTURE?

To end on such an idealistic note might seem not only starry-eyed, but banal, were it not that Yehuda Halevi's prophecy of the transience of the glorious Jewish life of medieval Spain has come true with a vengeance. Not many of us may be capable or desirous of echoing in our lives these words of Yehuda Halevi: "Servants of time are slaves of slaves, But the Lord's servant is truly free. Each man prays for his part in life, But my part, O Master, in Thee I see" (Baron's rendering). In this period of an increasingly secular Judaism, these lines may be emptied of their religious meangin and given new meaning in the context of Jewish culture (hardly anything but religious!) and of the renaissance of the Jewish nation in the State of Israel. Even so, the verses offer not only a challenge, but perhaps even a solution, or at least the seeds of a solution.

We have seen how intricately the fortunes of Israel were linked with the great Islamic civilisation in the past. It would be foolish to give credit for this on the whole beneficial state of affairs to the spiritual affinity of Judaism and Islam alone. Material factors played their full part no less. But, looking back, the historian can claim that neither of the two unequal partners was the loser. Judaism and Islam in their life together under a largely tolerant Muslim rule demonstrated beyond doubt that there was sufficient material and spiritual common ground between them to make this co-existence possible, and what is more valuable and important, even fruitful for others as well. We need only remember the legacy of this co-existence to the Christian West and modern Europe and beyond.

He would be a bold man who dare prophesy what the future holds in store for the very much needed co-existence of Israel and the Arab States on an equal footing, equal politically no less than culturally. I can only vary words I have used earlier to the effect that political and economic self-interest is not enough to lead to peaceful co-existence, let alone fruitful co-operation for the good of the Middle East and the world at large. Let us leave Great Power politics aside and assume hopefully, but unrealistically, that Israel and her Arab neighbours, now still hostile to her, are left a free hand to settle their differences by mutual agreement and friendly accommodation. Would it be possible to forge anew the link existing for many centuries from 622 C.E. onwards between the Jewish father and his son who has outgrown him, but has not undergone such fundamental changes that they could not work together on a common basis of a religious ordering of life on similar lines?

The answer is complicated through a not entirely dissimilar development of Judaism and Islam under the challenge of modern relativism and materialism. This is not conducive to a quick adjustment of a system built on absolute values—which are no longer recognised by many—

to new spiritual forces as yet not offering a solid basis for national and international development and co-operation.

We are rightly concerned about reform, the reform of rabbinic Judaism in Israel and in the *Galut*, and the reform of Islam in face of nationalism and technocracy. The one hopeful factor is perhaps that there are still Jewish and Muslim attitudes and ideas abroad in modern Jewish and Arab life as a live legacy from the past; perhaps they can be harnessed to bring about a coming-together for political and economic reasons if the destructive force of a virulent nationalism unmindful of its religious foundation and erstwhile content is not too strong.

This battle of adaptation of a religious culture, which has been losing ground among the leaders and the new generation in some Arab States which have won independence in our time, is still in full swing. I may be wrong in my conviction that, unless past memories come to life and infuse the struggle for consolidation and development of the newly-won freedom with a spiritual force which makes for more than material progress, little hope exists for stable peace and co-operation. These past memories which have gone from the minds of the younger generation with the waning hold of Islam are still present in many convinced Muslims who are loyal to the past and wish to make Islam the determining force in their national life. Only if they succeed in winning the allegiance of the secular minds to an Islam both traditional and progressive so that Muslim ideals can permeate and invigorate national life, only then is there a good prospect of a dialogue between Jews and Arabs that may lead—and we fervently hope will lead—to an end of the present dangerous impasse.

S. Landshut rightly pointed out that antisemitism as we know it in the West is not known among the Muslims in the modern Arab States as a decisive factor in their attitude to their Jewish fellow-citizens. But the establishment of the State of Israel in 1948 has had a profound influence on Arab-Jewish relations in the Middle East and North Africa. The presence of Jews in these States is a factor to be reckoned with in any solution of the Israel-Arab conflict and in the internal position of Jewish communities. Landshut's useful and interesting survey was published in 1950, and, if anything, the Jewish position has become even more delicate and uncertain in subsequent years. We need only think of the Suez affair and its repercussions on Egyptian Jewry.

One thing, however, is certain. If we look at the number and distribution of Jews in that part of the world and compare Landshut's figures with those published by the Institute of Jewish Affairs in 1959 we realise what an important and beneficial part Israel has played in the intervening nine years. The total of eight hundred and fifty-six thousand Jews in the Middle East and in North Africa in 1950 had fallen to approximately one hundred and fifty thousand in 1959. Where else in the whole wide world could world Jewry have settled seven hundred thousand Jews who had been living in Arab surroundings and had shared with the Arab majority many features of social and economic life, except in the State of Israel? Only its gates are open to any Jew the world over who wants to settle there and contribute to the well-being of Israel by leading a useful life among his own people in freedom and dignity. The most generous philanthropic effort, even on the part of American Jewry, could not have settled a fraction of these hundreds of thousands of Jews anywhere else. And what is more, despite the present difficulties of integration of large numbers of Oriental and North African Jews into the life of Israel with its inevitable friction, no other country on earth could and would have welcomed every one of them as the Jewish homeland has done so spontaneously.

Nor is that all: once these hundreds of thousands have become an integral part of the new community rapidly shaping its own style of living in the Middle East, they will be able to contribute to the understanding of the modern Arab mentality which is so essential a preparation for the dialogue to come between Israel and the Arab States.

SELECTED BIBLIOGRAPHY

Arberry, A. J.: *The Koran Interpreted*. London 1955.

Baron: S. W.: *A Social and Religious History of the Jews*, Vols. III-VIII. Philadelphia 1957-58.

Encyclopedia Judaica, iv, viii, x; especially the articles "Koran" and "Islam".

Fischel, W. J.: *The Jews in the Political and Economic Life of Mediaeval Islam*. London 1937.

Geiger, A.: *Judaism and Islam* (Eng. tr. of original German *Was hat Mohammed aus dem Judenthum aufgenommen*, 1833). Madras 1898.

Gibb, H. A. R.: "Law and Religion in Islam" in: *Judaism and Christianity*, III, ed. E. I. J. Rosenthal. London, 1938.

Modern Trends in Islam. Chicago 1946.

Goitein, S. D.: *Jews and Arabs*. New York 1955.

Goldziher, I.: *Vorlesungen über den Islam*. 2nd ed. Heidelberg 1925.

Guillaume, A.: *Islam*. London 1954.

"Philosophy and Theology" in: *The Legacy of Islam*. Oxford 1931.

"The Influence of Judaism on Islam" in: *The Legacy of Israel*. Oxford 1928.

Guttmann, Jul.: *Die Philosophie des Judentums*. Munich 1933 (also a Hebrew edition Jerusalem 1951).

Halkin, A. S.: "Judeo-Arabic Literature" in: *The Jews*, ed. L. Finkelstein. Philadelphia 1949.

Hirschberg, H. Z.: *Israel in Arabia* (Hebrew) Tel-Aviv 1946. (Standard History of the Jews in Arabia from the destruction of the Second Temple to the Crusades).

Husik, I.: *A History of Medieval Jewish Philosophy*. Philadelphia 1946.

Katch, A. I.: *Judaism in Islam.* New York 1954. (Commentary on first three *Suras* of *Koran* showing Jewish sources).

Landshut, S.: *Jewish Communities in the Muslim Countries of the Middle East.* London 1950 (with an important bibliography).

Lewis, B.: *The Arabs in History.* London–New York 1954.

Rosenthal, E. I. J.: "Islam" in: *Judaism and Christianity* II, ed. H. J. Loewe. London 1937 (with bibliography to 1937).

"Mediaeval Judaism and the Law" in: *Judaism and Christianity,* III.

Griechisches Erbe in der jüdischen Religions philosophie des Mittelalters. Stuttgart 1960.

"Avicenna's Influence on Jewish Thought" in: *Avicenna: Scientist and Philosopher.* London 1952.

Schacht, J.: G. Bergsträsser's *Grundzüge des Islamischen Rechts.* Leipzig 1935.

The Origins of Muhammadan Jurisprudence. Oxford 1953.

Schirmann, J.: *Die Hebräische Übersetzung der Maqamen des Hariri.* Frankfurt 1930.

Hebrew Poetry in Spain and Provence (Hebrew).

Spiegel, Sh.: "On Medieval Hebrew Poetry" in: *The Jews.*

Vajda, G.: *Introduction à la Pensée Juive au Moyen Age.* Paris 1947.

L'Amour de Dieu dans la Théologie Juive du Moyen Age. Paris 1957.

INDEX

Note: The words ALLAH, CHRISTIANITY, ISLAM, JEWS, JUDAISM, KORAN, MOHAMMED and MUSLIM occur too frequently to be indexed.